MotoGP
IN CAMERA

Published June 2007

A catalogue record for this book is available from the British Library

ISBN 978 1 84425 436 1

Library of Congress catalog card no. 2007922001

Published by Haynes Publishing,
Sparkford, Yeovil, Somerset BA22 7JJ, UK
Tel: +44 (0)1963 442030
Fax: +44 (0)1963 440001
E-mail: sales@haynes.co.uk
Website: www.haynes.co.uk

Haynes North America, Inc.,
861 Lawrence Drive, Newbury Park,
California 91320, USA

Designed by Lee Parsons

Printed and bound in England by
J. H. Haynes & Co. Ltd, Sparkford

MotoGP IN CAMERA

THE OFFICIAL PORTRAIT OF THE 990cc ERA

Haynes Publishing

CONTENTS

A very different view of Craner Curves at Donington Park.
GIORGIO NEYROZ

MIRCO LAZZARI

FOREWORD

When I was riding in the early days it used to be a big deal to get an action picture of yourself. I had this vision of how I thought I looked on the bike and it wasn't until people started taking pictures of me that I could really see my style, critique it and see how I might improve it. I'd look at guys who won a lot of races and study what they were doing on the bike – breaking it down from every angle. Wayne Rainey was someone you could always study as an example of riding position and body weight, how he put his feet on the pegs and how he held the bars. I'd also look at guys who crashed a lot and try to work out what they might be doing wrong. That's one of the reasons why I love books like this.

ANDREW NORTHCOTT

I look back on the 990s as a really special era. The future is four-strokes and these are the machines that brought four-strokes back to Grand Prix racing. I loved the 990s because they were very physically demanding bikes and that suited my riding style. It wasn't always hard to do a single fast lap, but to handle one of those beasts for 30 laps at race pace definitely separated the riders, and I miss that, even though I enjoy riding the new 800s too.

A book like this is one of the best ways to tell the whole story of the 990s. When you see some of these pictures I don't think you need a lot of words. Motorcycle racing can be the most rewarding experience in the world and it can also be a cruel game, and this book does a good job of capturing both sides. That's what I like about the sport. Sure there are days when it's frustrating, but bike racing isn't for everybody and I think you can see perfectly in this book why some people race them and others are by the side of the track taking pictures. Enjoy it.

NICKY HAYDEN

World Champion 2006

YAMAHA
brembo
ÖHLINS

◀ The most memorable paint scheme of the 990 years, Yamaha's retro yellow used only at the 2005 Grand Prix of the USA.

ANDREW NORTHCOTT

THE 990 YEARS

MotoGP: the most significant change ever made to Grand Prix regulations

Until the first race of the MotoGP formula it was impossible to imagine a more complete, efficient racing motorcycle than a 500cc V4 two-stroke. Yet the first time the 500s appeared on track alongside the new MotoGP four-strokes they disappeared into the background. Instantly, what had been man-eating motorcycles with razor-edge power bands were reduced to the status of also-rans. Lap and race records were obliterated. Despite valiant rearguard efforts, notably from Alex Barros and Loris Capirossi, the days of the two-stroke were numbered and decades of accumulated knowledge of arcane subjects, such as the inner workings of carburettor jetting or reading the colour of piston crowns, became redundant. The age of electronics had come to motorcycle racing. ▶

▶ The relevance of four-stroke technology to the development of road-going motorcycles loosened the manufacturers' purse strings and all four Japanese manufacturers, plus Aprilia, committed themselves to MotoGP from the start, with Ducati joining in for the second year.

At first the new 990s were unruly brutes, snaking into corners as teams and riders reared on two-strokes struggled to cope with the new experience of engine braking. It took a while to perfect electronic control as well. Some early engine management electronics incorporated basic fly-by-wire systems that dialled in more throttle than the rider was expecting, often with painful consequences.

The dominant motorcycle of the 990 era was Honda's V5 RC211V, which sprang fully formed onto the grid at Suzuka. In the first two years of MotoGP only three out of 32 races weren't won by a Honda.

That was the background to Valentino Rossi's astonishing decision to leave the all-conquering Repsol Honda team and go, with most of his crew, to Yamaha. Why? He needed the challenge to maintain his interest in racing, as well as proving that in motorcycle racing the rider matters more than the machine. He succeeded in both ambitions and rewrote the record books.

The only other marque to win in the 990 era was Ducati. They stormed onto the scene in 2003 but became consistent challengers for victories midway through 2005. Loris Capirossi was ever-present in the Bologna factory's line-up and scored the factory's first pole position, rostrum finish and victory in just five races. Troy Bayliss returned to the Ducati MotoGP team for the very last 990cc race and led Loris home for Ducati's first ever one-two.

By Valencia 2006, the once unruly MotoGP machines had been tamed, although it still took a remarkable rider to extract their full potential. The 990cc capacity limit had been chosen to ensure that the new bikes could outpace the old 500 strokers, but no-one had expected it to happen so easily or so quickly. So after just five years, by no coincidence the average life of a racing engine design, the 990s were consigned to history.

This book is a record of the most significant five years in the recent history of motorcycle racing as seen through the lenses of MotoGP's photographers. Even in this age of on-board cameras on every bike and super slow-motion replays, there's still something irresistible about a well-conceived still photograph.

In this book, I have, with the co-operation of the photographers themselves, attempted to illustrate the 990 years not just with the type of breathtaking action shot all of them take every weekend but also with images that might not otherwise have made it into print. The photos are divided into records of each year's racing interspersed with collections of images that illustrate different aspects of MotoGP life. Hopefully, the selection will give you a new insight into a remarkable period of motorcycle racing.

When the decrease in engine capacity from 990 to 800cc was announced, Valentino Rossi opined that we would look back on the 990 years as a golden era and called the bikes 'monsters.' Not many would disagree.

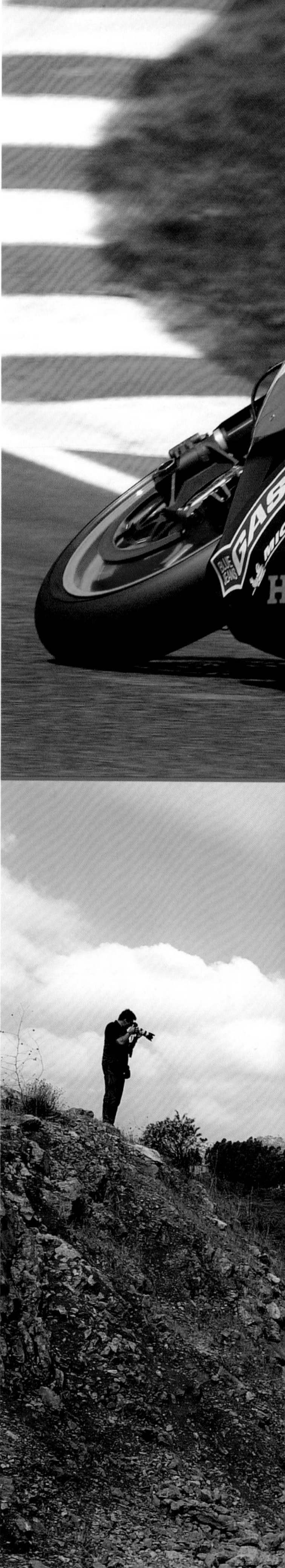

◄The combination of Valentino Rossi and Honda RC211V dominated the first two years of MotoGP.
ANDREW NORTHCOTT

▼Ducati had a lot to celebrate in the 990 years.
GOLD AND GOOSE

◄Not an obvious vantage point, but it secured the photograph on page 24.
HENK KEULEMANS

CINZANO
048
motogp

◀ Sometimes it's a matter of using your elbows as well as your camera.
PAUL BARSHON

The Photographers

Taking photographs is one of those jobs everybody thinks they could do. There can't be anyone who's been to a race meeting and never at some stage taken a photo of the action. Not so long ago everyone carried SLR cameras and used roll film, but now the world has gone digital. While the professionals still carry SLRs and long lenses, the fans in the stands use their phones.

Before the digital revolution, getting an image from camera to consumer was a complex and lengthy process often involving mobile darkrooms, despatch riders and early-morning vigils at the processing lab. Today, you can be looking at an image on your computer screen minutes after the photographer pressed the shutter release.

Technology has obviously eased the photographer's job in some ways, but it remains just as challenging to take a great picture. In fact the digital age has increased competition because electronics have enabled a lot more would-be snappers to produce work of decent quality with relative ease. Autofocus cameras mean that pin-sharp action photos in low light conditions are no longer rarities and readily available software can correct colour balance and density in a way undreamt of in the days of colour transparencies. Standing out from the background noise is just as difficult as ever.

Some of the contributors to this book have been shooting racing motorcycles since the 1970s, while others started after photographers stopped travelling with fridges full of Kodachrome. The images you see on these pages were selected by the men who took them. They're the pictures the photographers are most proud of, for a variety of reasons, as the skills involved in capturing them are extremely wide-ranging. Getting a crash shot, for instance, involves being in the right place at the right time and reacting instantly. The Danger chapter (page 116) contains a few examples of that combination of skill and luck. Of course, experience does tend to steer photographers to locations where something is likely to happen so the emphasis is on the skill side of that equation. By contrast, most of the photos in the Places chapter (page 32) had to be carefully planned. A photographer working alone will plan his race so that he can get a shot of the start or first corner, then move to a different corner or two before getting back to the pits for the rostrum. Agencies with more than one photographer at an event can afford the luxury of stationing one of their guys at an inaccessible location for just one shot.

How photographers work depends, of course, on who's employing them. Daily newspapers want uncluttered action shots; magazines prefer a bit more variety and space to superimpose headlines and type; a photographer working for a team must make sure he captures anything special that happens to their riders; and sponsors will want to see their banners and VIP guests in their pictures.

Like most jobs that require a rare blend of art and science, photography is easy to do badly and very difficult to do well. The contributors to this book do it very well indeed.

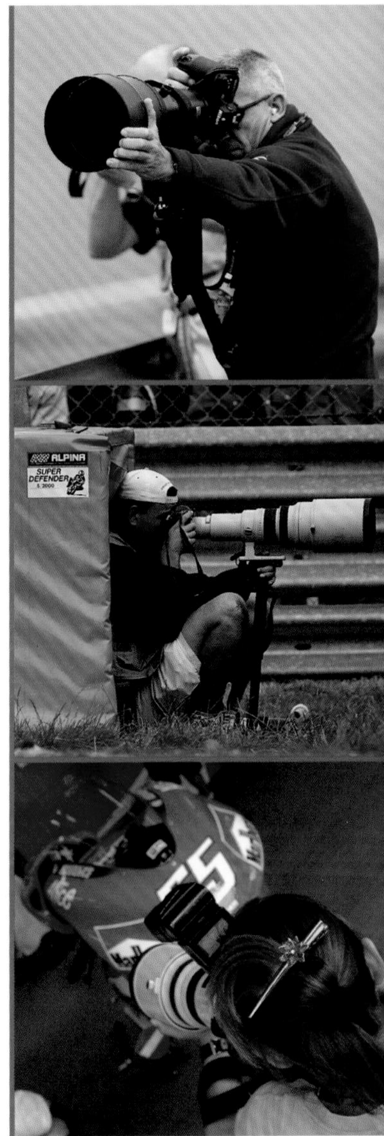

▲ Long lenses mean lots of glass – and lots of weight.
GERHARD RUDOLPH

▲▲ Hiding from the marshals can get you a new angle on the action.
GERHARD RUDOLPH

▲▲▲ Not every motorcycle photographer is a man, but not enough are female.
MIRCO LAZZARI

◀ Three photographers with but a single idea.
PAUL BARSHON

CONTRIBUTING PHOTOGRAPHERS

PAUL BARSHON

London-based Aussie who started snapping bikes full-time in 1995 and covered GPs from 2000 to 2004. Worked for Marlboro, Yamaha, Suzuki and Red Bull; founded the 2Snap agency with Friedemann Kirn and Graeme Brown. Nowadays concentrates on studio, advertising and brochure work.

www.paulbarshon.com

DAVID GOLDMAN

London-born founder of the Gold and Goose agency and a professional photographer since 1986. Gold and Goose now supplies magazines worldwide with pictures of MotoGP and the World and British Superbike Championships, as well as working for teams and sponsors.

www.goldandgoose.com

GARETH HARFORD

From York, Gareth started as a photographer's assistant, then, direct from college, joined Double Red to work on the British Superbike Championship. In MotoGP he has worked initially for 2Snap and latterly for Gold and Goose. He has been a professional for six years.

www.ghphotos.co.uk

MARTIN HEATH

One of the few solo operators, as opposed to agency men, around today. From Kent in the south of England, ten years a professional working mainly for British magazines and newspapers. Also works for the Kawasaki MotoGP team.

www.martinheath.net

PATRIK LUNDIN

Born in Gavle, Sweden, Patrik joined Gold and Goose in 2001 as a picture researcher with a background in editorial photography. Started photographing bikes the same year, and has covered every GP since 2002.

www.goldandgoose.com

MILAGRO

The Italian agency with the confidence of Valentio Rossi, headed by Gigi Soldano, a GP photographer for 20 years. Regular contributors include Fabrizio Porrozzi, Tino Martino and Stefano Taglioni. Clients include Italian newspapers and magazines, Ducati, Valentino Rossi, his team and sponsors.

www.photomilagro.com

JEAN-AIGNAN MUSEAU

A photographer for 25 years but nowadays he just takes pictures at weekends as his day job is sports editor of the French weekly *Moto Revue*. He shoots MotoGP, endurance, enduro and trials for work, and wildlife for pleasure.

GIORGIO NEYROZ

Started his career as a travel photographer in his native Aosta Valley in northern Italy. Moved to Formula 1 and was for four years official photographer of the Pharaohs Rally. Came to MotoGP in 2003 working for Dorna and the Italian Sort Image agency.

www.farefoto.com

HENK KEULEMANS

The longest-serving inhabitant of the MotoGP press office. Worked as a mechanic for world champion Lazzarini in the mid-1970s with fellow Dutchmen Jan Thiel and Martin Wijwaart of Jamathi fame. Started working for *Moto73* magazine in 1974 and still contributes, as well as working for Arai and the Dutch TT organisers. Addicted to Austin A30s.

SHIGEO KIBIKI

Has been a GP photographer since 1974. Works for *Riders Club* magazine in Japan. Kibiki-san is from Kyoto and road raced himself for seven years when he helped develop Kent Andersson's 125 Yamaha. Ignored team orders at Tskuba for his first – and last! – win.

FRIEDEMANN KIRN

Australia-based German, who worked first as a newspaper journalist then picked up a camera. Has always worked for *Motorrad*, the top European motorcycle mag. One of the founders of the 2Snap agency.

www.2snap.com

MIRCO LAZZARI

An Italian from Imola, 21 years a professional photographer working in Formula 1 and Italian domestic racing. Has been shooting MotoGP since 2002 for the Italian Grazie Neri agency and Gold and Goose in the UK.

www.mircolazzari.com

ANDREW NORTHCOTT

Contracted photographer for HRC – if you see an official Honda racing picture, Andrew took it. Also works for magazines in the UK, Germany and the USA. Aussie-born, he lives in Texas with his American wife, Olivia, and their two children, Annelise and Stirling.

www.ajrn.com

STAN PEREC

Started on football before discovering bikes in 1972. Since then has shot endurance and GP for Elf, Honda, Gauloises Yamaha and Rothmans France among others. Nowadays works for *L'Equipe* and PSP. The Polish-born doyen of the French media.

www.photostanperec.com

GERHARD RUDOLPH

Has photographed endurance, Superbike and GP over the last 25 years but nowadays works mainly for German magazine *Motorradfahrer*. Lives in Ingelheim, rides a Honda CB1300 and has a fondness for Laverdas.

LUCASZ SWIDEREK

Warsaw based, but influenced by and working with his great uncle Stan Perec. Ten years a photographer, started working at the Polish Championship, and now works mainly for PSP and Polish magazine *Swiat Motocykli*.

www.photoswiderek.com

◀ The first moments of the first MotoGP race. The field rushes towards Suzuka's first turn led by Olivier Jacque on Yamaha number 19, but he is about to be overwhelmed by Shinichi Itoh's Honda (72), Akira Ryo's Suzuki (33) and Carlos Checa's Yamaha (7).
SHIGEO KIBIKI

RACING 2002

Honda and Rossi dominate the beginning of the four-stroke era

No-one really knew what would happen when the lights went green at Suzuka for the first race run under the MotoGP formula. Although the new 990cc four-strokes had dominated practice (but not by a huge margin), the old 500cc two-strokes still outnumbered the new bikes. Three 990s lined up on the front row alongside Loris Capirossi's V4 Honda stroker, and it was another 500, Olivier Jacque's Yamaha, that got off the line best. Moments later though, the truth of the new formula was demonstrated: Jacque's two-stroke was swamped by a stampeding mob of bellowing four-strokes.

The new 990s monopolised the rostrum at Suzuka, the first two-stroke (Norifumi Abe's Yamaha in fifth place) being over 20 seconds behind Valentino Rossi's ▶

▶ victorious Repsol Honda. If the weather had stayed dry, lap and race records would have been obliterated.

Although the two-strokes were more nimble and could carry more corner speed, the 990s just marched past them as soon as throttles were opened. Through the season the two-stroke riders would continue to do well in qualifying when they could maintain momentum in the corners, but in a real live race they found it almost impossible to overtake. No-one had expected the new bikes to be so dominant so quickly.

At Suzuka four-stroke representation was only two Hondas, two Suzukis, two Yamahas and a lone Aprilia (plus Honda and Suzuki wild cards) in a field of 22. The riders were Valentino Rossi and Tohru Ukawa (Honda), Max Biaggi and Carlos Checa (Yamaha), Kenny Roberts and Sete Gibernau (Suzuki) and Regis Laconi (Aprilia). The have-nots instantly started agitating for an increased supply of four-strokes.

What happened when new supplies arrived was instructive. Daijiro Kato rode a Honda V5 in anger for the first time at the Czech GP. He only just missed out on pole to Biaggi and finished second behind him in the race. Alex Barros got a Honda V5 for Motegi and promptly won (after Rossi had tied up the title with four races to spare), and then did it again in the finale at Valencia.

You did need a Honda to make an impression. The RC211V won 14 of the 16 races (Biaggi and Yamaha triumphed in the Czech Republic and Malaysia). It débuted at Suzuka looking like the finished article – that was doubly impressive as the Honda was a completely new design whereas Suzuki and Yamaha started by putting new motors in old two-stroke chassis. Aprilia were the most innovative: their triple used fly-by-wire electronics and pneumatic valves direct from F1 but the team didn't have the resources to field more than one rider or develop their brutally powerful machine. Yamaha started with an undersized engine and carburettors because they didn't think the tyres would handle the full potential of a 990 motor, but Michelin's new-generation 16.5-inch S4 rubber made that worry redundant and Yamaha improved their bike considerably through the season. However, the factory fell out with lead rider Biaggi and the divorce was finalised well before the end of the year.

Suzuki hadn't intended to field their 990 until 2003 but advanced their plans under pressure from the team. Their V4 looked a bit like a toolroom special next to the slickly finished Honda and it lacked top-end power, but Roberts (and wild-card Akira Ryo) got it on the rostrum in wet conditions. Kawasaki made it a full house of Japanese factories for the last four races of the year.

The technical subject that exercised the designers most wasn't tyres or power output, but engine braking and how to manage it. Slipper clutches underwent a rapid evolution but with varying degrees of electronic control and aids such as electronically varied tickover or throttle kickers on one or two cylinders. It wasn't uncommon to see bikes fishtailing into corners as the combined electrical and mechanical systems failed to limit what we all learned to call back torque.

▼Valentino Rossi had cause to celebrate: 11 wins in the season and the first MotoGP title to add to his 125, 250 and 500 crowns.

GOLD AND GOOSE

◄Alex Barros got a Honda V5 for the last four races of 2002 and enjoyed himself hugely. Here he awaits the final race of the year in Valencia, where he beat Valentino Rossi on the last lap.

ANDREW NORTHCOTT

▼Kawasaki debuted their ZX-RR Ninja at Motegi. Test rider Akira Yanagawa did not have an easy time.
ANDREW NORTHCOTT

▶ The Sachsenring should have seen the final hurrah of the two-strokes, but a late mistake by Alex Barros braking for the first corner saw the Brazilian crash and scoop up the luckless Olivier Jacque.
GERHARD RUDOLPH

2002 TIMELINE

7 APRIL
First MotoGP race: Rossi wins at Suzuka on a Honda, with wild card Akira Ryo second on a Suzuki and Carlos Checa third on a Yamaha.

21 APRIL
South African GP, Welkom: Loris Capirossi is the first man to put a 500 on the MotoGP rostrum with third place on a Honda.

5 MAY
Spanish GP, Jerez: Daijiro Kato gets his first rostrum in the top class with second on a two-stroke Honda.

18 MAY
French GP, Le Mans: for the first time all of the riders qualifying on the front row are on four-stroke machines.

1 JUNE
Italian GP, Mugello: during practice Regis Laconi's Aprilia becomes the first MotoGP bike to break the 200mph barrier.

20 JULY
German GP, Sachsenring: Olivier Jacque sets pole position on a two-stroke Yamaha.

25 AUGUST
Czech GP, Brno: Max Biaggi and Yamaha are the first to beat Honda's V5. Kato scores a rostrum finish in his first ride on a four-stroke.

21 SEPTEMBER
Rossi clinches the first MotoGP title at Rio with four races to spare.

6 OCTOBER
Pacific GP, Motegi: Alex Barros gets a V5 and promptly wins first time out. His team-mate, Capirossi, angry at being passed over, scores the last ever rostrum finish by a two-stroke 500. Kawasaki début their MotoGP machine in the hands of Akira Yanagawa.

19 OCTOBER
Australian GP, Phillip Island: Jeremy McWilliams leads an all-two-stroke front row on the Proton, but gets blown into the weeds – along with Garry McCoy, Nobuatsu Aoki and Jürgen van den Goorbergh – before the first corner on race day. McWilliams' pole is the last for a two-stroke in the MotoGP class and the first for a rider on Bridgestone tyres.

Arai
HELMET
WWW.SU
Team
SUZUKI
MOTORCYCLE TOP FASHION LEADER
MICHELIN
SUZUKI
#1
RYO
SUZUKI
NANKAI RACING
NR
SUZUKI
NANKAI RACING
NR

Suzuki's development rider Akira Ryo got on the rostrum at home in Japan using Dunlop tyres. The team switched to Michelins early in the season and Ryo made five more points-scoring appearances but didn't get on the rostrum again.
GOLD AND GOOSE

▲ Max Biaggi and his Yamaha skirt the rocky landscape of Estoril in testing for the Portuguese GP.
GOLD AND GOOSE

▲ Aprilia's Cube was the most technically adventurous MotoGP machine, but it was far from easy to ride. Even tough guy Regis Laconi had trouble wrestling it into submission.
GOLD AND GOOSE

'Maybe we are lucky to ride these bikes because soon they will become legend'

Valentino Rossi

REPSOL
GAS
HONDA

Carlos Checa leads a multi-coloured freight train around Donington Park during MotoGP's first visit to the UK. Valentino Rossi, Max Biaggi, Kenny Roberts, Olivier Jacque, Norrick Abe and the rest follow.
GOLD AND GOOSE

Marlboro
YAMAHA
3

◀Some race tracks fool the spectator into thinking they could do what the guys on track are doing. Not Phillip Island: watch racing motorcycles at the Australian GP and you understand the level a GP racer operates at. This is Max Biaggi heading for the splendidly named Siberia corner.
GOLD AND GOOSE

▲Max Biaggi radiates tension as he prepares to do battle with a horde of Honda V5s.
GOLD AND GOOSE

AGV
46
Drudi Performance
arnette
REPSOL
GAS
GASJEANS.COM
HONDA
MANPOWER
NGK
SPARK PLUGS
HONDA
REPSOL
REPSOL

The Doctor is in. Valentino Rossi on his way to winning at home at Mugello. The one-off crash helmet design echoes his dad Graziano's colours, and the icons around the base pay tribute to various aspects of Italian life.

SHIGEO KIBIKI

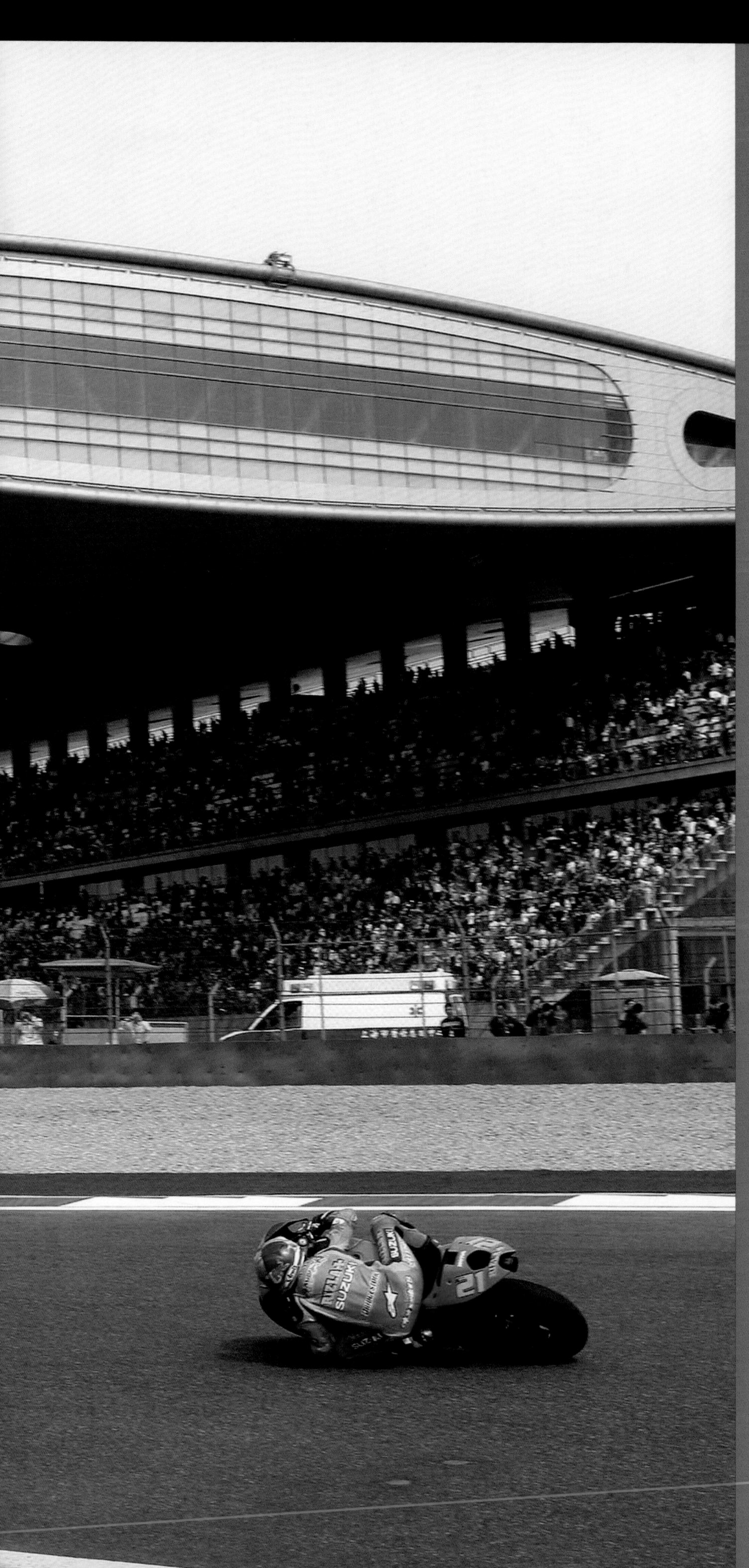

◀ The giant wings of the Shanghai International Circuit dwarf Colin Edwards and John Hopkins. The wing in the distance contains the press office, and the one in the foreground various other parts of the administration. The little open-air balconies are for smokers.
ANDREW NORTHCOTT

PLACES

The racing stays constant but the settings and surroundings vary enormously

MotoGP has travelled to six of the seven continents: Europe, Africa, Australasia, Asia, North and South America. If someone had built a race track in Antarctica then MotoGP would have gone there too. Only one track – Assen in the Netherlands – has hosted a Grand Prix every year the World Championship has existed, but other circuits with their roots in the classic and pre-war eras of racing, such as Donington Park, are still on the calendar. Both Brno and Barcelona used to run Grands Prix on closed-roads circuits but nowadays their races are held on exemplary modern circuits that have been purpose-built with both rider safety and spectator convenience in mind.

When a country doesn't have a circuit or any ▶

▶ history of motorcycle racing, then it has to build a new venue. Malaysia, China, Turkey and Qatar have done just that. The first three were primarily intended for Formula 1, so they feature some stunning architecture and construction on a grandiose scale, with money no object. At the other end of the economic scale Valencia built for a comparative pittance a stadium circuit that squeezes the maximum amount of tarmac into the minimum area. Sometimes a new track manages to combine the old and the new, like the Sachsenring, which no longer shares any of the original road circuit's layout but has reminders of the area's history and engineering prowess preserved everywhere.

The new Spanish circuits and the Shanghai International Circuit are built on the edge of industrial estates on the outskirts of big cities, so if you prefer a scenic setting you have to go to the older tracks. Donington is based on the perimeter road of a British country house, complete with sweeping lawns; Laguna Seca looks over the Monterey Peninsula on California's Pacific coast, one of the most beautiful places on Earth; Phillip Island is on the Bass Strait between mainland Australia and Tasmania; and Mugello is in a valley in the Tuscan hills just outside Florence, thus combining racing, scenery and cultural overload in one location.

Paddock regulars are often asked the best place to go and see a MotoGP race. It's an impossible question to answer simply because there's no such thing as a bad place to see a MotoGP race...

◄ Qatar isn't desert as westerners usually understand it. It's flat, rocky, covered with a layer of fine dust – and empty. And in the middle of this emptiness you suddenly come across a race track.

HENK KEULEMANS

▲ The Jacarepagua circuit at Rio shares its back straight with the banked oval circuit. Somehow the scale seems all wrong for motorcycles.

GOLD AND GOOSE

‘That’s the first corner I ever got my elbow down on with a qualifier – and stayed on...’

John Hopkins

► The vast acreage of painted concrete on the inside of La Caixa corner at Catalunya is a favourite of photographers. This shot uses the giant lettering to form the perfect diagonal with John Hopkins’ Suzuki – just like the photography magazines always tell you to.
LUCASZ SWIDEREK

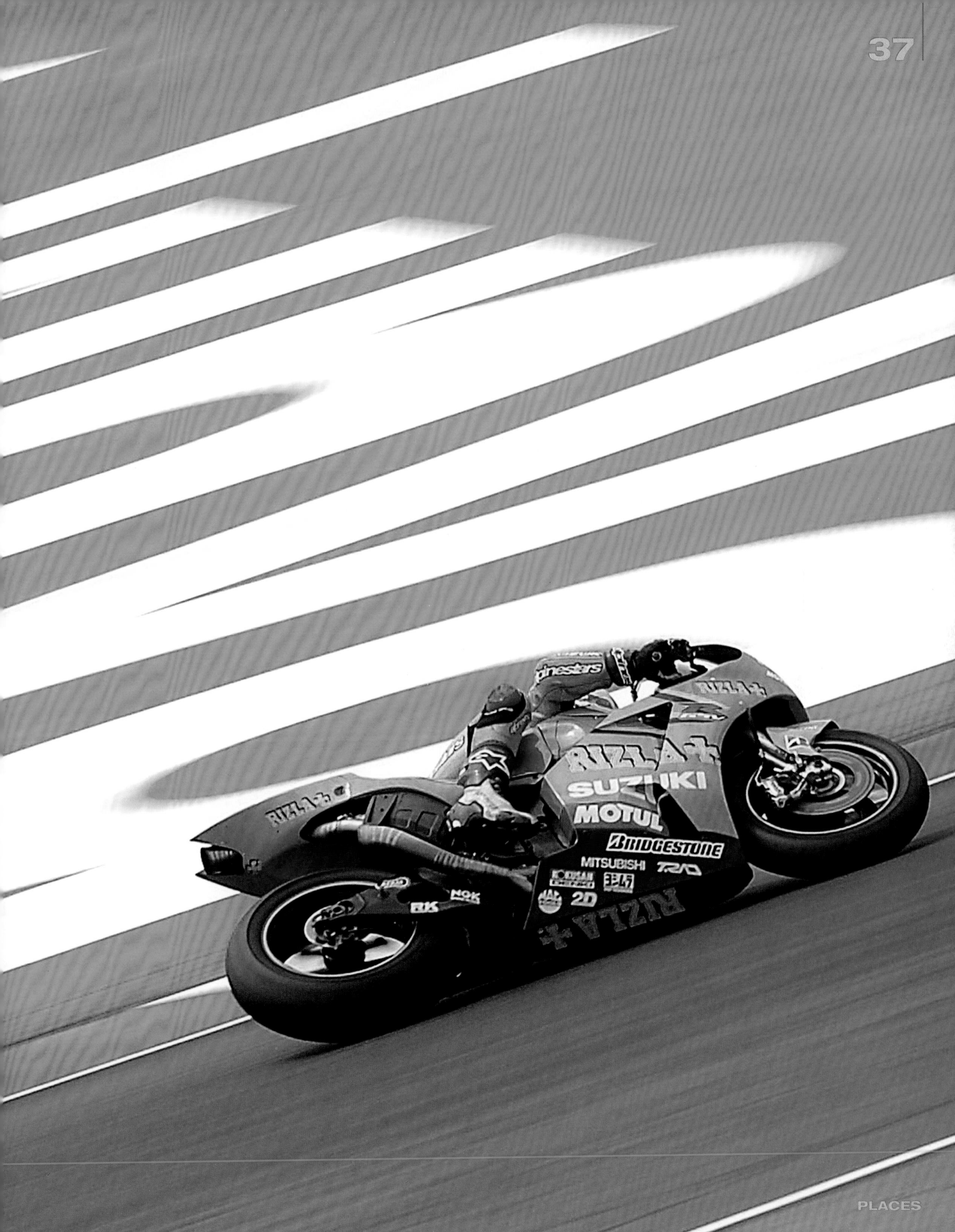

RIZLA+
SUZUKI
MOTUL
BRIDGESTONE
MITSUBISHI
2D
NGK

▼The Jerez circuit celebrates Spain's greatest ever motorcycle racer, 13 times world champion Angel Nieto, with this statue as well as a corner named in his honour. The 12+1 on wheels refers to Nieto's legendary superstition about the number 13.

HENK KEULEMANS

►A flat landscape and old-fashioned, big-wheeled, sit-up-and-beg pushbikes? It could only be Holland and the Assen marshals' transport.

GERHARD RUDOLPH

▲ The finest sight in British racing – the pack sweeping down the Craner Curves at Donington Park in front of a full house and the Spitfire. This stretch of tarmac would feature in any attempt to construct the perfect circuit from the best corners in the world.

PAUL BARSHON

Overleaf This aerial shot of Valencia shows exactly what the phrase 'stadium circuit' means: packing two and a half miles of tarmac into the smallest possible area so that every spectator can see all the action.

MARTIN HEATH

Power

► Fast food in Japan is a bit different from the burger vans we're used to in Europe, and doubtless better for you too.
GOLD AND GOOSE

▼ When you get to go to Rio you must do the sights. Only Carlos Checa didn't take the tourist bus: he rock-climbed to the top of the Corcovado, with its iconic statue of Christ the Redeemer and stunning view of the Sugarloaf.
PAUL BARSHON

► The tunnels under Twin-Ring Motegi's oval circuit let photographers play with some unusual lighting. This wide shot shows exactly what's going on but a close-cropped shot can look very strange indeed.
GOLD AND GOOSE

▼The traditional gateway to the Shanghai paddock and the water garden on the left make an extreme contrast with the mammoth, modernistic construction of the pitlane building.
HENK KEULEMANS

▼ If you turn left when you go through the gate in the picture on the opposite page, this is what you come to. The teams' offices at the Shanghai International Circuit are built on stilts over a lake bordered by elegantly planted gardens. It makes for a scenic ride to your pit garage.
ANDREW NORTHCOTT

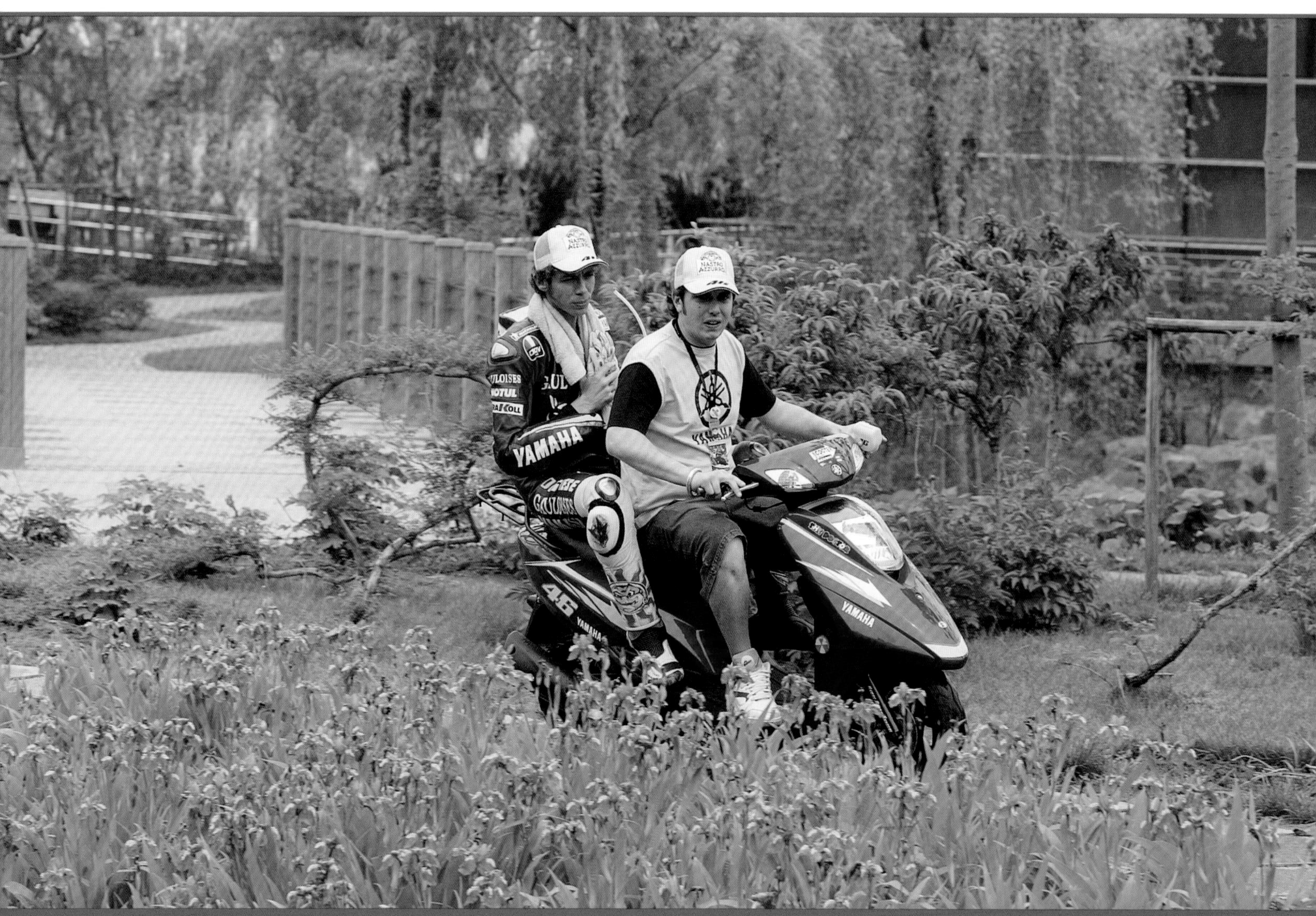

'Here nature and technology are carefully used to create harmony between the elements'

Hermann Tilke

◀ If there was a prize for best architectural design at a MotoGP track, it would go to the Sepang F1 Circuit's grandstand and particularly the 'bird's wing' roof.
GOLD AND GOOSE

▲ The glass-fronted offices above the Catalunya pitlane provide an opportunity for photographing mirror-image reflections. This shot of Sete Gibernau works so well because the photographer has caught him coming past his crew on pit wall.
GOLD AND GOOSE

GAS
GAS
GAS
GAS
GAS
GAS
GAS
GAS
GAS

The Istanbul Park circuit is arguably the best of the new purpose-built tracks from a pure racing point of view, but it's also a spectacular piece of architecture.
ANDREW NORTHCOTT

▼The German GP is one event where you don't go without a ticket. All three days are sold out just weeks after the previous event – which explains why the campsite on the hill occupies a larger area than the track itself.
ANDREW NORTHCOTT

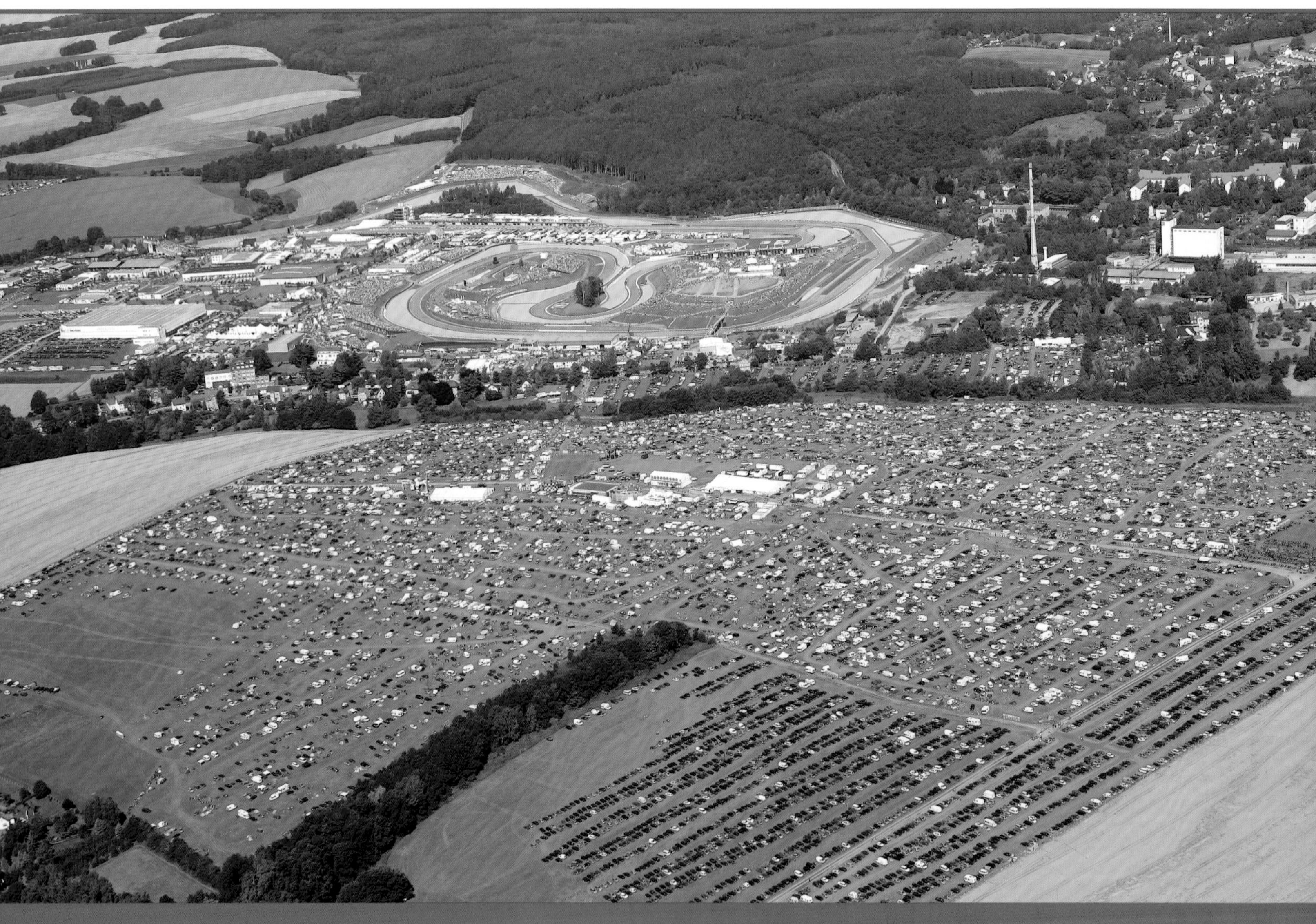

'We brought the race track to the people, the whole area is crazy for racing'

Alex Hofmann

▼The Sachsenring is a track of two halves: there's a high-speed downhill that ends the lap and a first half like this – a twisty run down to the Omega and back up again between steep banks and vertiginous grandstands.
GERHARD RUDOLPH

Red Bull
U.S.
GRAND PR

Grand Prix motorcycle racing returns to the USA, and this is the first lap of the 2005 MotoGP race at Laguna Seca. This view from the outside of the first corner is popular with photographers but the waving flags give this image an extra dimension.
GIORGIO NEYROZ

Marlboro
65
Marlboro
Marlboro
DUCATI
Marlboro

◄ Loris Capirossi slides the Ducati Desmosedici around Barcelona on the way to the factory's first win in the top class of motorcycle racing. The previous time Ducati won a GP had been in 1959 (the 125cc race in Ulster thanks to Mike Hailwood) and it was 27 years since an Italian had won on an Italian bike – that was the legendary combination of Giacomo Agostini and MV Agusta at the Nürburgring in 1976. The heat haze in this shot shows just how much heat the motor was throwing out – Ducati had to modify the bodywork to avoid cooking their riders.
MARTIN HEATH

RACING 2003

Rossi dominates, Ducati arrives, Kato departs

The death of Daijiro Kato in the first race of the year was, first and foremost, a private tragedy for his family. It also robbed Japan of an exceptional rider who many believed would be the country's first champion. He was the only rider whose times Valentino Rossi regularly checked when he came back to his pit.

Kato's death also had a profound effect on his team-mate Sete Gibernau and the rest of Team Gresini. They arrived in South Africa traumatised after the funeral in Japan, but Sete offered the best possible tribute to number 74 by taking pole position and a hard-fought win. More than that, he seemed to find something deep within his character that launched him on a quest to dethrone Rossi. For 2003 they managed to remain friends despite Sete ►

being the only man who could regularly give Valentino a hard time. On occasion, as in Germany, Sete won the race in a fair fight but once again Rossi won the title with races to spare. His win in Australia, where he overcame a ten-second penalty for a yellow-flag infringement, is without doubt one of The Doctor's most remarkable victories and ranks with the best of any champion you care to mention. The fact that it came on the fabulously fast curves of Phillip Island made the ride even more breathtaking.

One would have expected Honda's advantage from the first year of MotoGP to have been eroded 12 months on, but the other Japanese factories lost the plot and what challenge there was came from newcomers Ducati. The Italian V4 was fast from the word go, putting Loris Capirossi on the rostrum in the first race and on the front row at the second. At the third race, Capirossi and team-mate Troy Bayliss qualified first and second. Three races later Loris made history by winning the Catalan GP. The other newcomer was Bridgestone and the Japanese tyre company achieved its first MotoGP rostrum with Makoto Tamada in Rio.

The Rookie of the Year title went to young American Nicky Hayden, who had so nearly signed for Yamaha before being tempted away to be Rossi's team-mate in the Repsol Honda works team. The ex-dirt-tracker took a little while to adapt and inherited his first rostrum when Tamada was controversially excluded for barging past Gibernau at Motegi. His second rostrum came at Phillip Island thanks to breathtaking passes on first Tohru Ukawa and then Gibernau on the fast run to Lukey Heights. No wonder Yamaha were annoyed about losing him. They replaced Max Biaggi with 250cc champ Marco Melandri and brought in the vastly experienced Brazilian rider Alex Barros. Although Barros was the fastest man in pre-season testing, Yamaha's optimism was soon extinguished. The company's only rostrum of the year came from Barros in the wet in France. Melandri's season was ruined by a nasty injury suffered in the very first practice session for the very first race of the year, and Barros was also injured in Japan.

Aprilia brought in Colin Edwards (and Michelin tyres) from World Superbikes and partnered him with Noriyuki Haga. Sixth in the first race looked promising but it never got any better for Aprilia's quixotic triple. There was a lack of development parts to cure the obvious problems, and ever-louder rumours about the company's poor financial state meant it was no surprise that 2003 turned out to be Aprilia's last year in MotoGP.

The WCM team also ran out of sponsorship money but got round it by the novel expedient of building their own bike, which promptly fell foul of the FIM's technical regulations on using production parts so they wheeled out some of their old two-strokes for a few races. You didn't have to be small to find out how difficult it was to compete with Honda's V5. Kawasaki arrived full-time in 2003 but their 'super-superbike' design failed to get a sniff of the rostrum and the regular riders, Garry McCoy and Andrew Pitt, only got in the points six times.

Rossi took full advantage of his rivals' disarray. When he finished he was always on the rostrum. He started from pole nine times, won nine races, took 14 fastest laps (12 of them new records) and accumulated a record points tally. Then he announced that he was going to leave Honda and join Yamaha. As shocks go this was very high on the sporting Richter scale.

▼The most emotional win of the 990 era: Sete Gibernau salutes his lost team-mate Daijiro Kato after winning the South African GP at Welkom.

MILAGRO

◀Italian joy is unconfined on the Barcelona rostrum: Loris Capirossi soaks Ducati technical director Corrado Cecchinelli as they celebrate the Desmosedici's first MotoGP win after just six races.

MARTIN HEATH

▼Makoto Tamada and Bridgestone tyres arrived in MotoGP full-time. The combination got on the rostrum twice in the season, in Brazil and Japan, only to be disqualified from Tamada's home race. It was a promising début season for both rider and tyre company.

GOLD AND GOOSE

►Rookie of the Year Nicky Hayden scored two rostrum finishes towards the end of 2003 but his all-action, back-it-in style excited fans everywhere. This shot could only be from Phillip Island, scene of Nicky's best ride of the year.

GOLD AND GOOSE

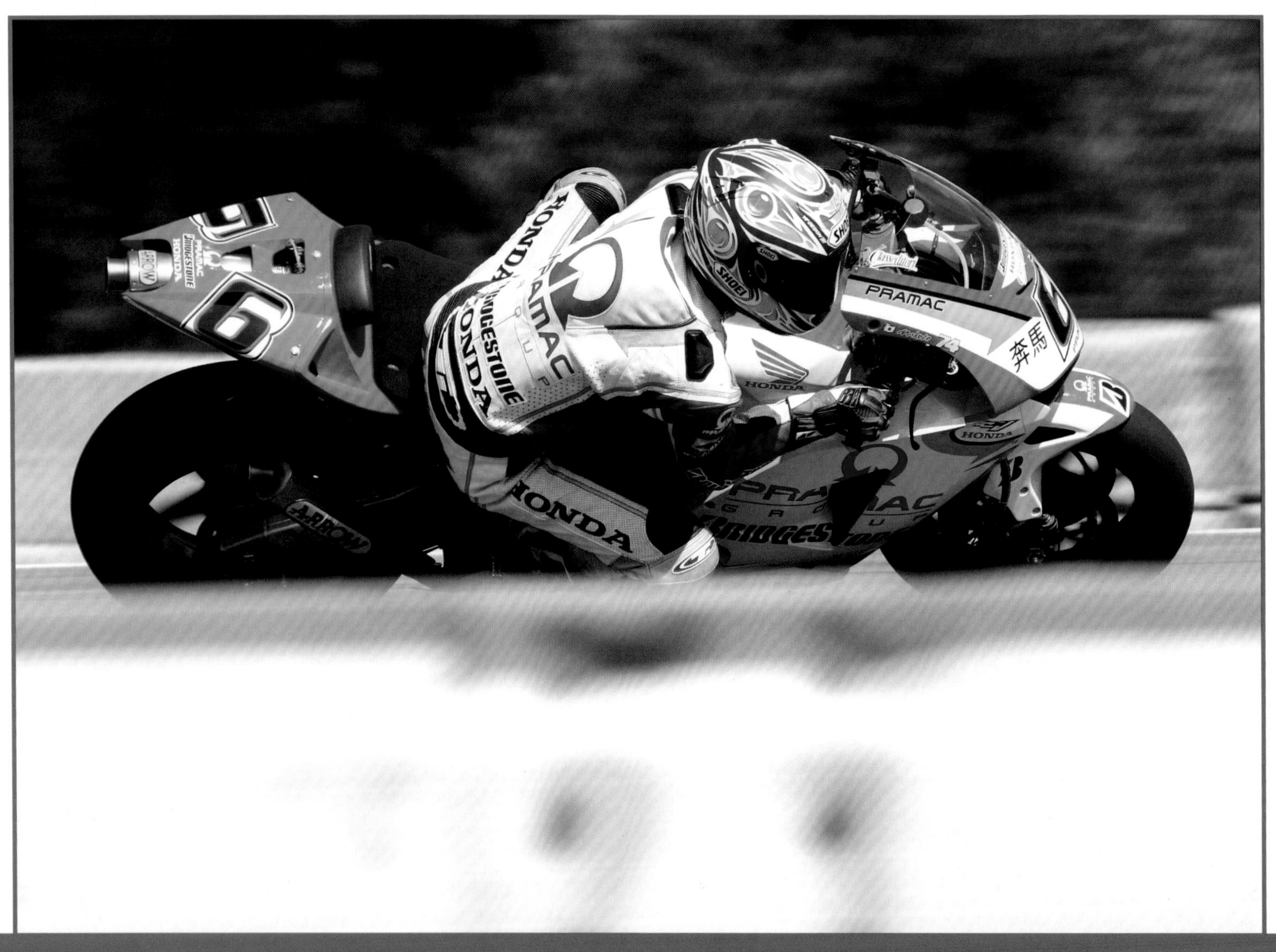

2003 TIMELINE

6 APRIL
Japanese GP: Japan's champion-in-waiting, Daijiro Kato, dies after crashing at the end of the third lap. Ducati get on the rostrum with third place in their first race with the Desmosedici four-stroke.

10 MAY
Spanish GP: Loris Capirossi gives Ducati their first ever pole in the premier class.

23 MAY
French GP: Team Roberts début their own V5 four-stroke in practice but revert to their 500 for the race.

25 MAY
French GP: First use of new rain rules designed to do away with aggregate races sees the race restarted as a 13-lap dash. Sete Gibernau wins, Alex Barros in third gets Yamaha's only rostrum of the season.

8 JUNE
Italian GP: Valentino Rossi's victory at Mugello was the 151st for Italy in the premier class, making it the most successful nation in terms of GP wins.

15 JUNE
Catalan GP: Loris Capirossi takes Ducati's first win in the premier class.

17 AUGUST
Czech GP, Brno: Chris Burns becomes the last ever rider to race a two-stroke in the MotoGP class.

20 SEPTEMBER
Rio GP, Jacarepagua: Bridgestone tyres get their first MotoGP rostrum finish courtesy of Makoto Tamada, who finished third on a Honda.

5 OCTOBER
Pacific GP, Motegi: Tamada is disqualified for an innocuous last-lap pass of Gibernau, thus promoting Nicky Hayden to his first top-three finish – although he didn't get to stand on the rostrum.

19 OCTOBER
Australian GP, Phillip Island: probably Rossi's greatest race. He gets a 10sec penalty for a yellow-flag infringement but still wins the race, by 15secs (ie, 5secs after the penalty). Hayden leads a race for the first time – and also stands on the rostrum for the first time.

2 NOVEMBER
Valencian GP: Rossi's last race for Honda. He wins it sporting a one-off Austin Powers paint scheme designed by the winner of a magazine competition.

'You try to use a lot of corner speed, then hold it flat stick, then button it back if things get a bit dicy'

Garry McCoy

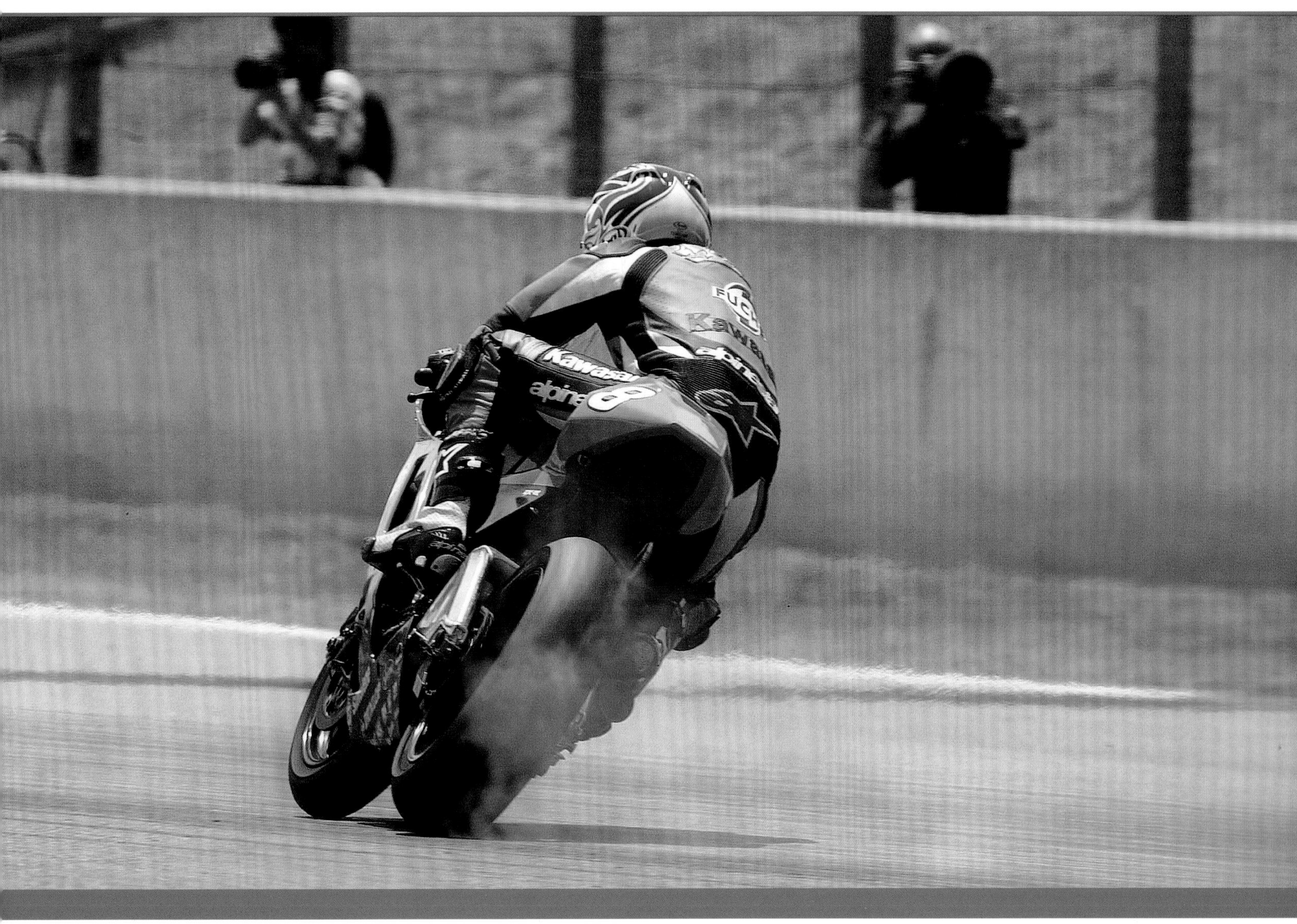

▲ One second in the life of a tortured Dunlop slick. The Kawasaki team didn't have a happy year but Garry McCoy was always worth watching, as can be seen in this sequence from Catalunya. This image is made up of three exposures from an eight-frame sequence butted together. Nothing in the image has been computer-enhanced; that smoke is real.
ANDREW NORTHCOTT

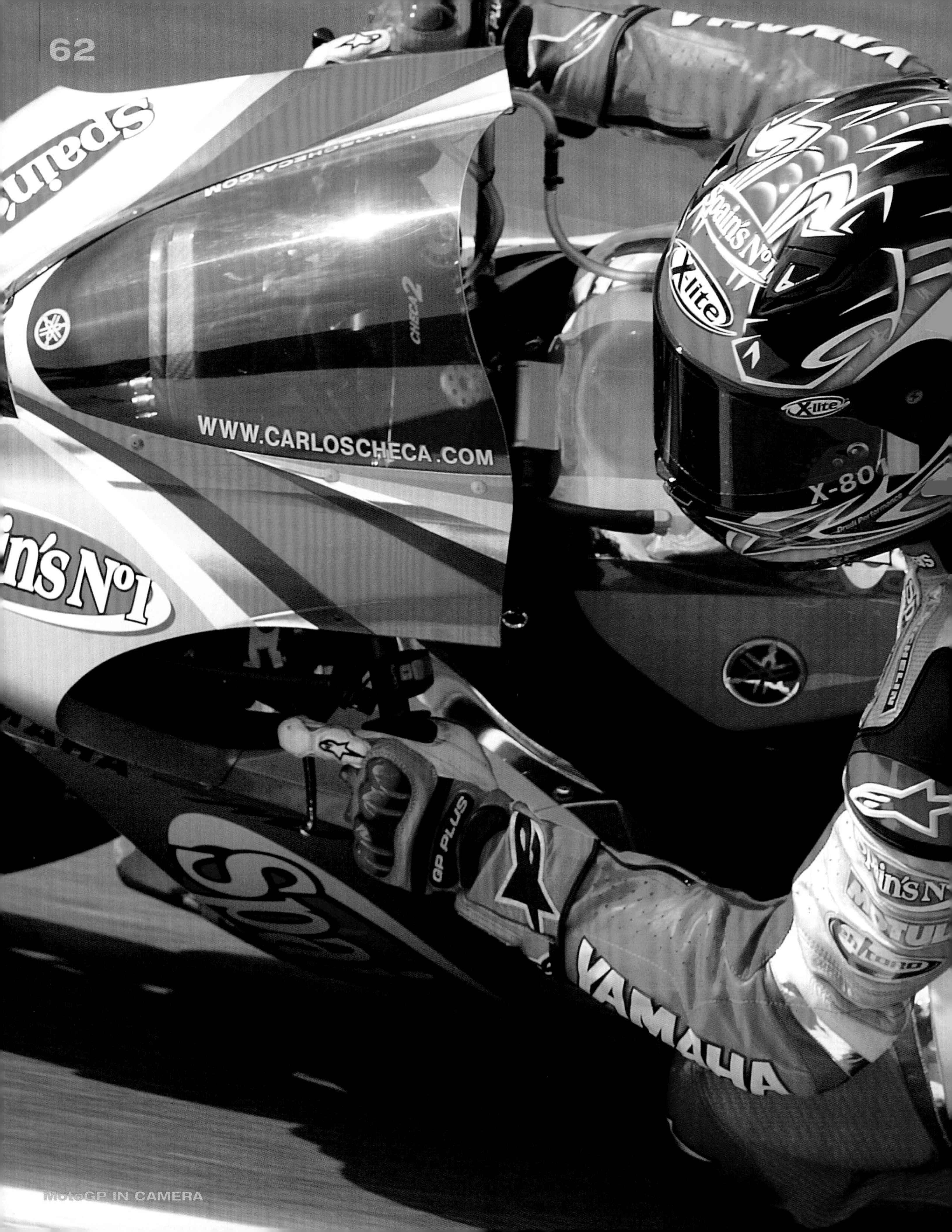
WWW.CARLOSCHECA.COM
X-lite
X-lite
X-801
GP PLUS
YAMAHA

Carlos Checa started every race of the 990 years on a four-stroke, riding and scoring top-three finishes on both Yamaha and Ducati. Valentino Rossi was also ever-present, as was Shinya Nakano although he rode two-strokes for all but three races of the 2002 season.
GERHARD RUDOLPH

▲ A scene from Valentino Rossi's greatest race? The leaders of the Australian GP sweep down towards Honda Corner, where Rossi later overtook Marco Melandri under a yellow flag and attracted a 10sec penalty – but he went on to pull out a 15sec margin. As the man himself later suggested, perhaps this could only have happened on the magnificent sweeps of Phillip Island.
GOLD AND GOOSE

▲ Bring on the big guns; Max Biaggi awaits the start on his V5 Honda.

PAUL BARSHON

► Nine times out of 16 races in 2003, Valentino Rossi's number 46 marker reminded him to start from pole position.
PAUL BARSHON

▲ Valencia: Valentino ignores all distractions as he contemplates his last ride on a Honda.
GOLD AND GOOSE

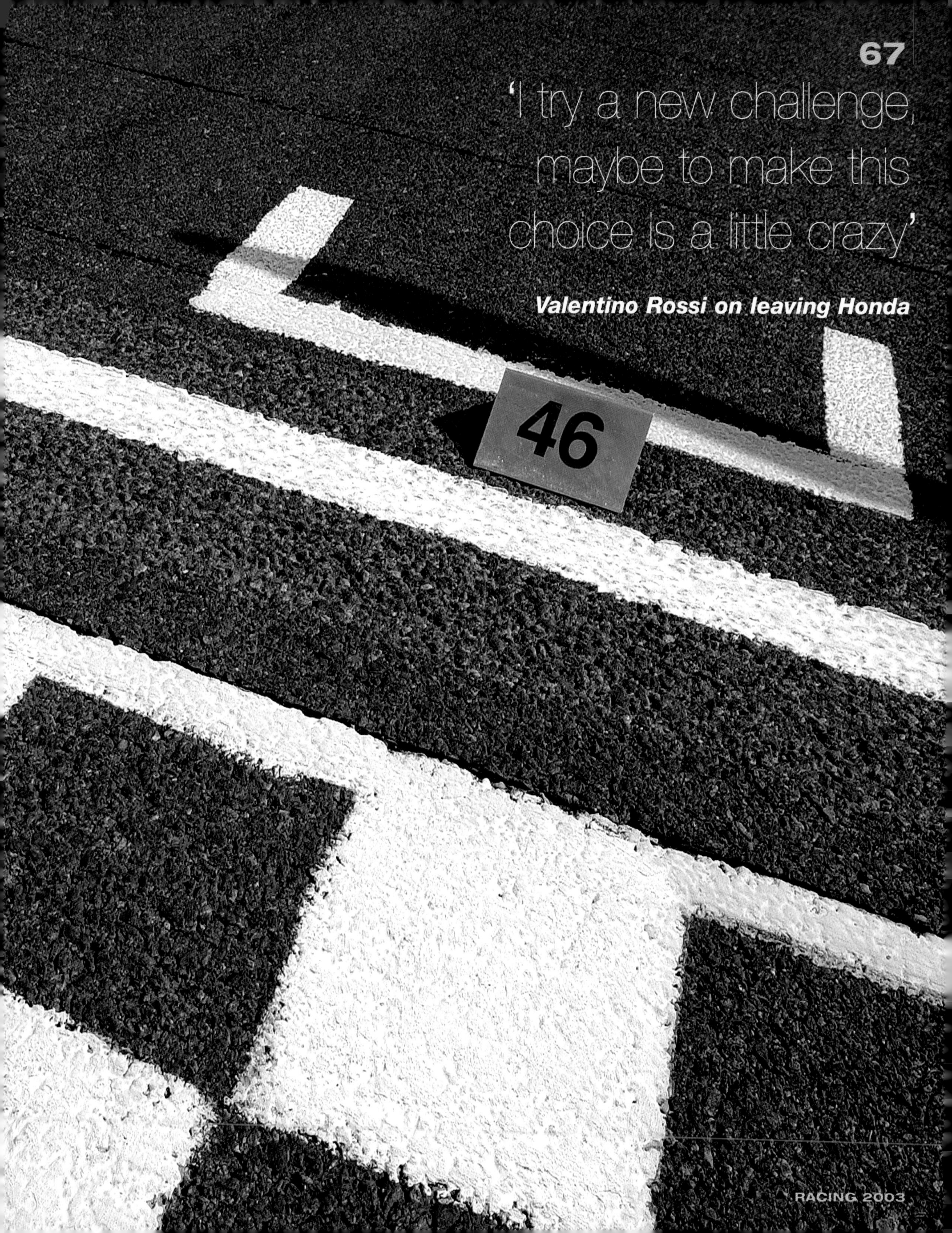

'I try a new challenge, maybe to make this choice is a little crazy'

Valentino Rossi on leaving Honda

agv
Drudi Performance
arnette
TRIBÙ DEI CHIHUAHUA
THE DOCTOR
REPSOL
GAS
MANPOWER
NGK
BLUE JEANS GAS
HONDA
REPSOL
GAS
DAINESE
RC211V
REPSOL
HONDA HRC

SHOEI
HONDA
MoviStar
alpinestars
Telefonica
MoviStar
HONDA
Castrol
MICHELIN
brembo

KATO

▼The death of Kato touched fans everywhere. Banners like this appeared at tracks all over the world, not just at Motegi.
FRIEDEMANN KIRN

▼Racers paid tribute to Kato by carrying his race number on their bikes, leathers and helmets. It will only be used again in MotoGP with the express permission of his family.
GERHARD RUDOLPH

▲The razzmatazz of racing didn't sit well with Daijiro. A devout Buddhist, he appeared happiest with his young family, and had an astounding ability to sleep anywhere.
MILAGRO

▲Kato only had seven races on the four-stroke Honda but got on the rostrum at Brno, set pole position at Motegi and finished seventh in the championship.
MILAGRO

►Daijiro Kato definitely would have won MotoGP races, but would he have been World Champion? Most insiders believe he certainly would have taken the fight to Valentino Rossi.
GERHARD RUDOLPH

Piolanti
Spain'Nº1
caffè
MoKadOR
SHOEI
Spain
'Nº
Telefonica
Movistar

KATO

◀ A striking image – a low-angle view of Valentino Rossi's Official Fan Club making a lot of noise.
MARTIN HEATH

FANS

For racing to be atmospheric, grandstands need to be packed

Watching a race on television is all very well, but nothing beats being able to say 'I was there'. The shared experience of watching a race in the company of tens of thousands of other enthusiasts is something that stays with you. Even the discomfort of watching Rossi in the rain at Donington Park fades with time and all you remember is the spectacle and the noise. That is due to a mixture of factors, chief of which is that elusive factor called 'atmosphere', and that's down to you and your fellow fans.

MotoGP bikes are loud but even a gridful can't overpower the noise the Jerez crowd makes when a Spanish rider hits the front. Latin fans seem keen on noise: at Mugello bikes are fitted with giant ▶

▶ megaphone exhausts, in Spain fans bring in motors from garden equipment. It's different in the Far East. At Motegi and Suzuka you learn that the polite round of applause that greets a rostrum from Tamada or Nakano is the Japanese equivalent of the storm of noise that greets Checa, Gibernau or Pedrosa in Barcelona. Politeness also rules at Laguna Seca where the fans who buy paddock passes can be heard calling riders 'Sir' and apologising for bothering them for an autograph.

The giant grandstand at Assen has been known to break into football-style chants and singing, and when Jürgen van den Goorbergh led the first lap of a restarted wet race they nearly took the roof off. At Sepang you can hear 40,000 people sigh in sympathy with a fallen rider. At the Sachsenring the music on the PA is stuck in the 1970s and you can't get a ticket for love or money. At Phillip Island the crowd contains more hardcore bikers than anywhere else – all stockman's coats, Harleys and straggly beards. China doesn't yet attract a big crowd but those who are there make a disproportionate amount of noise – and then you understand why when you go into Shanghai and are assailed by the world's loudest waiters and pushiest salesmen.

A motorcycle racing fan can go to any of these places and know he will find kindred spirits without the need for a common language. We're all fans of the sport of motorcycle racing.

◀ Nowhere is motorcycle racing more popular than in Spain, and no riders are more relentlessly in the media spotlight than the Spanish. Sete Gibernau coped with the pressure better than most.
MIRCO LAZZARI

▲ Not every race track has grandstand seats for all. The ancient art of wire-hanging is demonstrated at Le Mans.
GERHARD RUDOLPH

◀ Spanish race fans tend to be uninhibited, but even by their standard this guy could be considered extreme; at least he took the blade off the chainsaw.
PAUL BARSHON

▲ Anyone who has been to Assen over the years knows this feeling. When it rains, the banking at Assen is turned into a sea of polythene, as experienced spectators come prepared.
PAUL BARSHON

It can get lively in the Assen grandstands. More fans from more countries gather at the Dutch TT than any other event. It's the only race to have been in the Grand Prix calendar continuously since the inception of the World Championships back in 1949.
PAUL BARSHON

CIRCUIT ASSEN
YAMAHA

► The hillsides of Mugello are staked-out by the fan clubs of the Italian riders. The highest point of the track, on the outside of Turn 3 (Poggio Secco), is turned yellow by supporters of number 46.

MILAGRO

▼ Somehow or other, year after year, this Flintstones tribute vehicle gets onto the Mugello track ten minutes after the end of the race – and always in the correct colour scheme.

GERHARD RUDOLPH

▶ It's tough spectating at Motegi. First there's the three-hour drive out of Tokyo. Then there's getting your Asimo autographed – Honda's long-term robot project is made much of at the Twin Ring. At least this young fan got his Rossi hat and T-shirt before it all became too much.
PAUL BARSHON

▼Messages of support for Yamaha's riders at Motegi in the usual baffling Japanese mix of cute cartoons and T-shirt slogan English.

PAUL BARSHON

▼ Ducati paint the house red: Mugello's Correntaio grandstand is filled by the people who make and ride the red bikes from Bologna.
MILAGRO

'The bike seems to run better on Italian air'

Livio Suppo – Ducati team manager

Some fans know how to get Valentino Rossi's attention...
HENK KEULEMANS

...and there are many ways of showing support for your favourite rider.
GERHARD RUDOLPH

THE NURSE

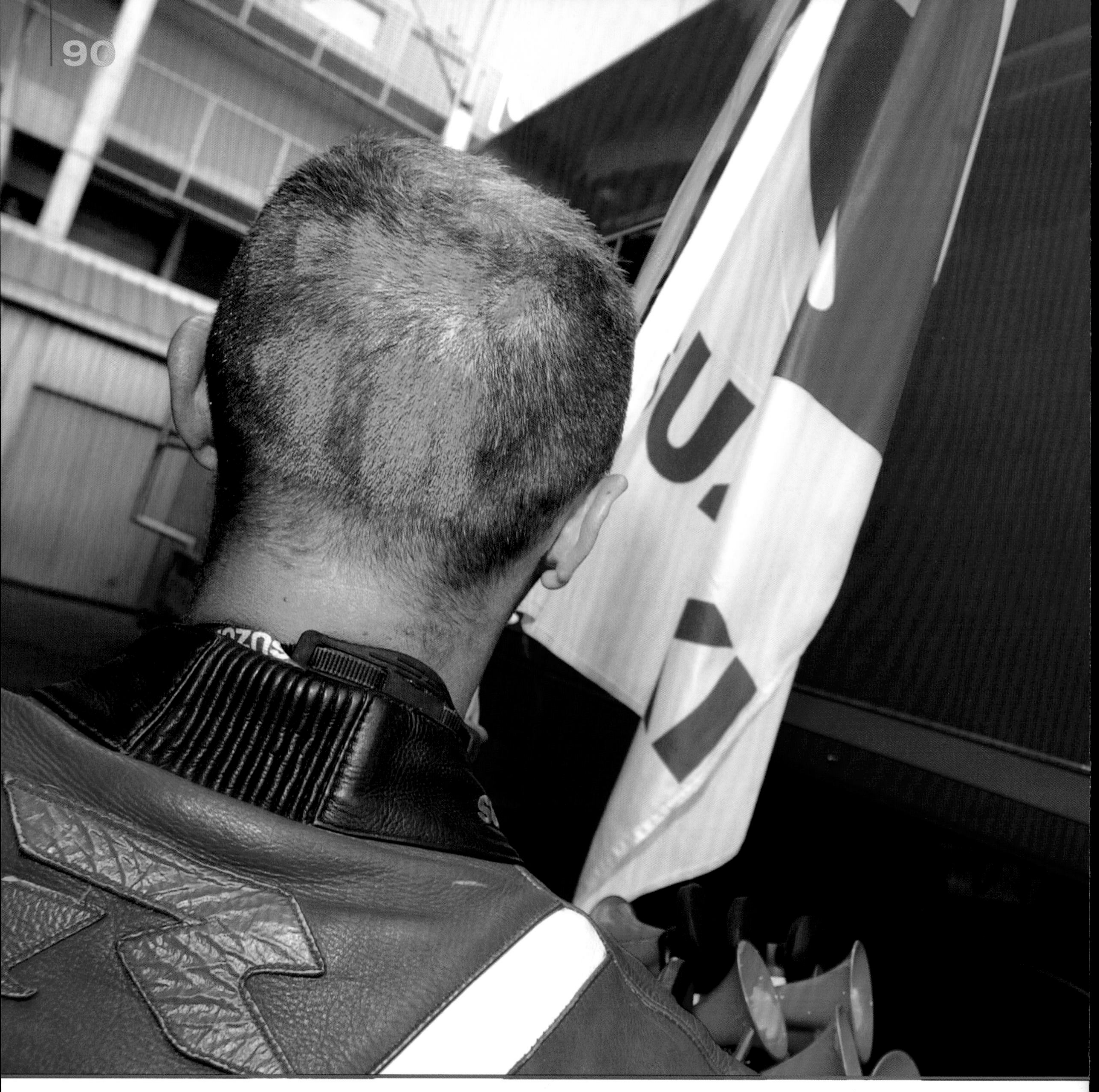

▶ Every race is a home race for Valentino Rossi – as these noticeably non-Italian flag-waving fans at Motegi demonstrate.
PAUL BARSHON

◀ Got the bike, got the matching leathers, got the flag – now how else can I show my devotion to the Suzuki cause? A Kenny Roberts fan waits patiently for a glimpse of his hero.

PAUL BARSHON

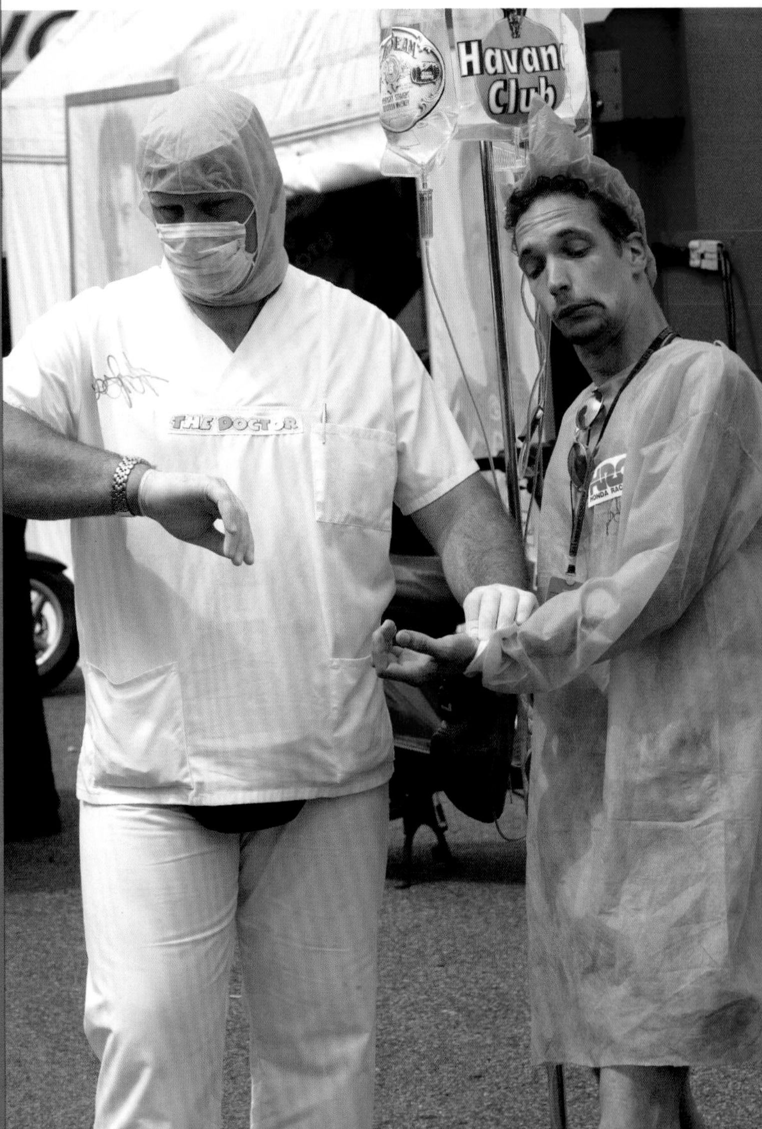

▲ These guys are not on the staff of the Clinica Mobile... fans of Doctor Rossi have been known to indulge in some intricate theatricals to gain entry to the paddock.

PAUL BARSHON

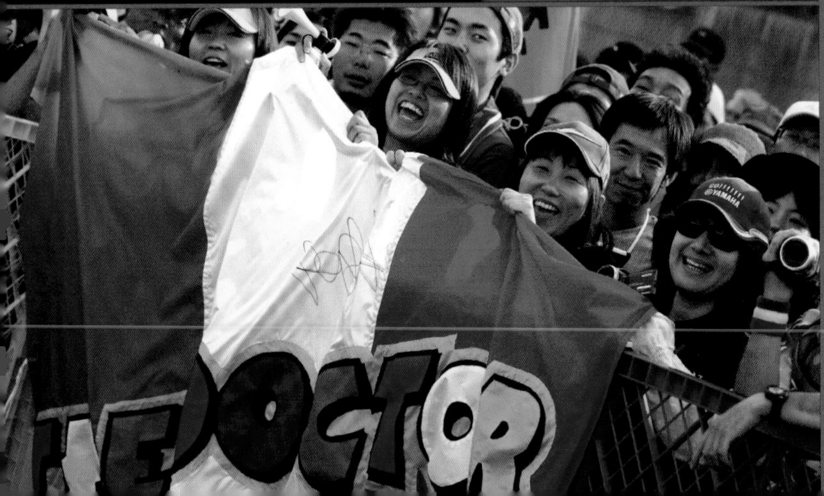

Rossi escapes Mugello's 2002 post-race track invasion by the skin of his teeth. Unfortunately the fans got on track on the slowdown lap and a serious incident was only narrowly averted, leading to increased security in subsequent years.
MILAGRO

GAULOISES

◀New season, new bike. Valentino Rossi walked out on the all-conquering Repsol Honda team to join the under-achieving factory Yamaha squad. Sixteen races later there was no doubt that only Mike Hailwood rivalled him for the status of the greatest ever.
HENK KEULEMANS

RACING 2004

Rossi turns to Yamaha, wins again and touches greatness

Anyone harbouring lingering doubts about Valentino Rossi's place in the pantheon of motorcycling gods had them utterly quashed by one of the most remarkable seasons of racing ever. For 2004 Valentino left the all-conquering Repsol Honda team and joined Yamaha, a factory seemingly in terminal decline. Pre-season all the talk was of when he would be able to challenge for a rostrum place and then for a win. Most estimates started at half-season for the rostrum and didn't even contemplate a victory.

It's important to remember that Yamaha had never gone so long without a rostrum and that no-one had ever won back-to-back races in the top class on different makes of bike, so Rossi's win at the first race, in Welkom, after a ▶

▶ Both Makoto Tamada and his Bridgestone tyres came on in leaps and bounds. The combination was good enough to win two races and set pole three times. However, the tyres could not match Michelin at many tracks, so Tamada was unable to mount a title challenge on his Honda.

GOLD AND GOOSE

▶ thrilling battle with Max Biaggi, was truly historic. As well as ending Yamaha's unenviable run, he beat Giacomo Agostini's record run of 22 consecutive podium finishes and equalled Barry Sheene's feat of winning the opening race of four successive seasons. By retaining his title he made it four championships in a row in the premier class, something only Ago, Mike Hailwood and Mick Doohan had done. Only Geoff Duke and Eddie Lawson had won titles on different makes of bike, and only Eddie did it in consecutive seasons. It was Yamaha's first title since Wayne Rainey won in 1992, and Valentino scored more points and won more races in a season than any other Yamaha rider before him.

None of this would have been possible without Jerry Burgess, the race engineer Rossi brought with him from Honda along with his mainly Australian crew. Along with Masao Furusawa, who had already worked through some of the problems back in Japan, they re-engineered the Yamaha M1 into a winner.

Over the years, Rossi had grown tired of the Honda way of doing things. In his opinion they undervalued the rider's part in winning and this was a major element in his decision to move to a new team.

Rossi also discovered a new focus for his will to win. After his crew illegally cleaned his grid spot in Qatar, he was demoted to the back row. Rossi blamed Sete Gibernau and his team – for a second season the Spaniard had shown himself to be the only rider who could regularly take the fight to Rossi. 'He will not win another race,' said Rossi after crashing in pursuit of his new worst enemy. Next time out he destroyed the field to retain the title and celebrated by sweeping the track with a broom.

Yamaha may have benefited from the Rossi effect, but their other riders didn't even get on the podium (although Checa did set pole in Qatar). Honda, on the other hand, saw all six of their riders get on the podium, including Makoto Tamada, who gave Bridgestone their first win in MotoGP. That was in Brazil and came on the heels of Kenny Roberts and Suzuki giving the Japanese tyre company their first pole position. MotoGP now had a real tyre war on its hands; Bridgestone put a dent in Michelin's hegemony with two wins and four pole positions. As well as Tamada's Honda and the Suzukis, Kawasaki also used Bridgestone tyres.

The Kawasaki was undoubtedly the most improved bike of the year thanks to an Eskil Suter chassis, and the team was rewarded with their first MotoGP rostrum thanks to Shinya Nakano at home in Motegi. Ducati did not build on their impressive first year but saved their season with rostrums in the last two races. The small teams suffered too. Aprilia never got the new parts the squad was promised and by the end of the season the company's financial woes meant this would be the last season in MotoGP for the fearsome three-cylinder Cube. Kenny Roberts continued to battle on with his own V5 but slipped behind even the lesser factory teams – a disappointing conclusion to The King's expensive flirtation with Formula 1 technology. It looked, though, as if a more conventional route might open up. KTM gave up the idea of running their own MotoGP team but kept working on their engine. Team KR tested it and were mightily encouraged.

It's very easy to like Valentino Rossi, and even easier to be a fan. It is, however, very difficult to over-praise his achievements in the 2004 season. This was a year when he made doing the impossible commonplace.

▼Marco Melandri had a troubled second season in MotoGP but scored two rostrum finishes and got to sport this Spiderman livery in Portugal. The idea was that the fairing and Marco's kit would be auctioned for charity – unfortunately he crashed.

GOLD AND GOOSE

▲Max Biaggi and Sete Gibernau help Valentino Rossi to celebrate his historic win in South Africa.

STAN PEREC

2004 TIMELINE

18 APRIL
South African GP: Rossi wins his first race on a Yamaha, breaking the longest losing streak in the factory's history and beating Agostini's record run of 22 consecutive rostrum finishes.

2 MAY
The MSMA announces the first changes to MotoGP's technical regulations. Fuel tank capacity is to come down by 2 litres to 22 litres for 2005, and an engine capacity reduction from 990cc to 800cc is proposed for 2007.

6 JUNE
Italian GP: Shinya Nakano crashes at over 190mph on Mugello's front straight after his rear tyre delaminates. It's the fastest crash in GP history. Rain reduces the race to a six-lap sprint, resulting in the first serious suggestions that wet races should not be stopped.

13 JUNE
Catalan GP: Marco Melandri finishes third – his first rostrum in the top class.

26 JUNE
Dutch TT, Assen: Alex Barros becomes the first rider in Grand Prix history to start 200 races in the top class.

3 JULY
Rio GP: Kenny Roberts gives Suzuki their first pole position in MotoGP.

◀ Same team, different tyres: Biaggi and Tamada at Rio, heading, respectively, for second and first places on Michelin and Bridgestone tyres.

FRIEDEMANN KIRN

▼ Nobuatsu Aoki prepares to leave the Sachsenring pitlane on the Roberts V5. Team Roberts' brave attempt to design and build their own four-stroke motor finally came to nought and they tested KTM's motor before the end of the season

GERHARD RUDOLPH

4 JULY
Rio GP: Makoto Tamada gives Bridgestone their first win in the top class

25 JULY
British GP, Donington: Colin Edwards finishes second and stands on the MotoGP rostrum for

6 SEPTEMBER
Team Roberts test KTM's V4 engine on the Monday after the Portuguese GP

19 SEPTEMBER
Japanese GP: Shinya Nakano scores his and Kawasaki's first MotoGP rostrum finish

2 OCTOBER
Qatar GP: Rossi and Biaggi demoted to the back row of the grid for cleaning their grid slots. Gibernau and Edwards finish one-

17 OCTOBER
Australian GP: Valentino Rossi wins a frantic last-lap dice with his new enemy, Sete Gibernau, to retain his title and give

▼Winners usually look like they haven't had a hard day at the office but the heat of Malaysia is different. But it isn't just the heat that has affected Rossi; this was the race after the Qatar incident and he has just crushed the opposition and ignored Gibernau's proffered handshake. The eye contact is unusual and telling – something you only get from Valentino when the photographer is Italian.
MILAGRO

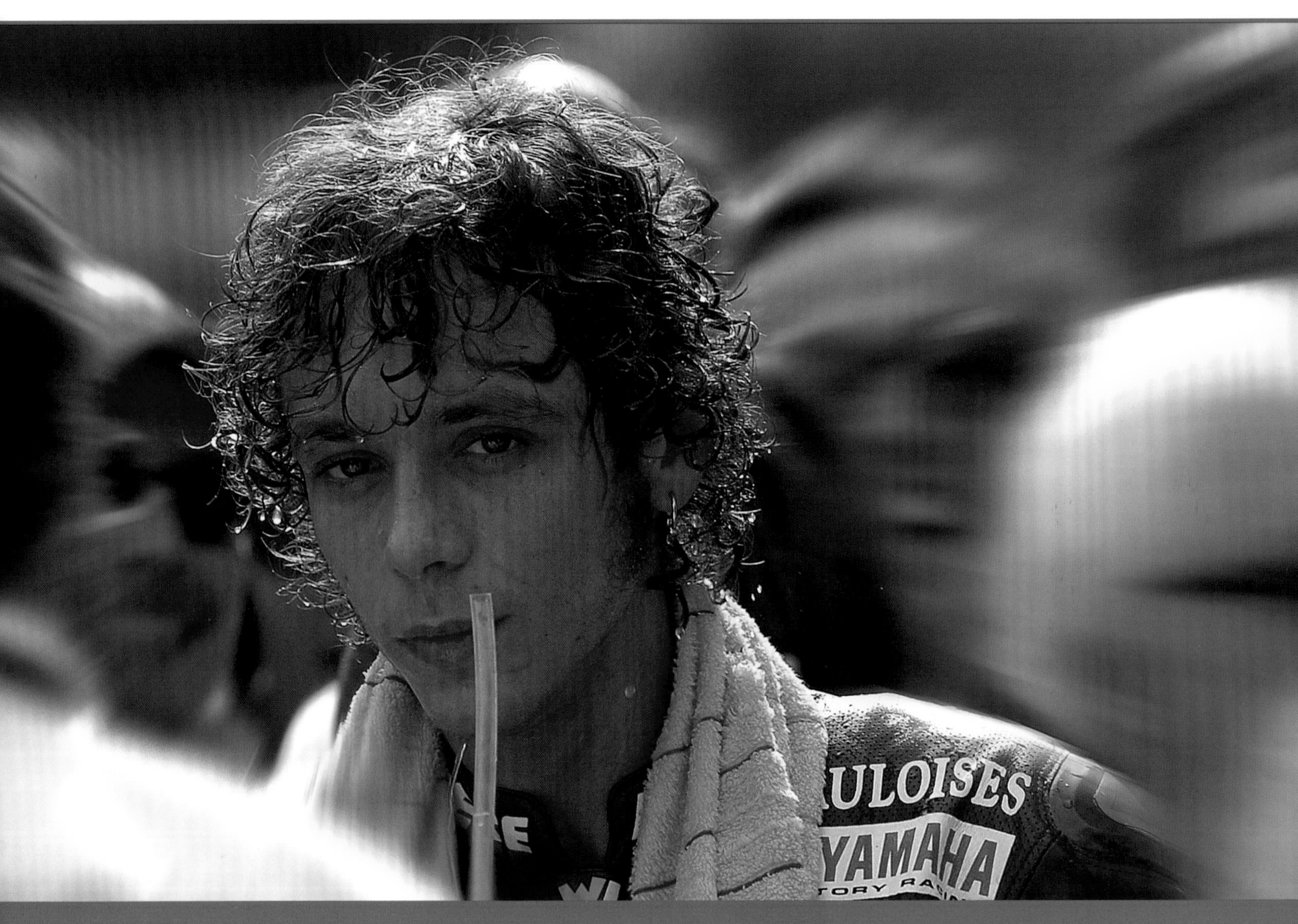

'Gibernau was fast, the battle was good'

Valentino Rossi

▼Once upon a time, dual-compound tyres were exotic rarities. Now, Michelin, Bridgestone and Dunlop produce tyres with different tread rubber for either side and a harder compound in the centre to handle 200-plus horsepower.
PAUL BARSHON

‘To win nine races, same as I did last year on Honda, is unbelievable’

Valentino Rossi

Rossi on his way to crashing in Rio.
PAUL BARSHON

▼ Racers have to absorb as much information in their pit garage as they do on the track. Every degree of throttle rotation, every gear change, every squeeze of the brake lever – it is all recorded, pored over and analysed to try and reduce lap times by a few hundredths or thousandths of a second.

PAUL BARSHON

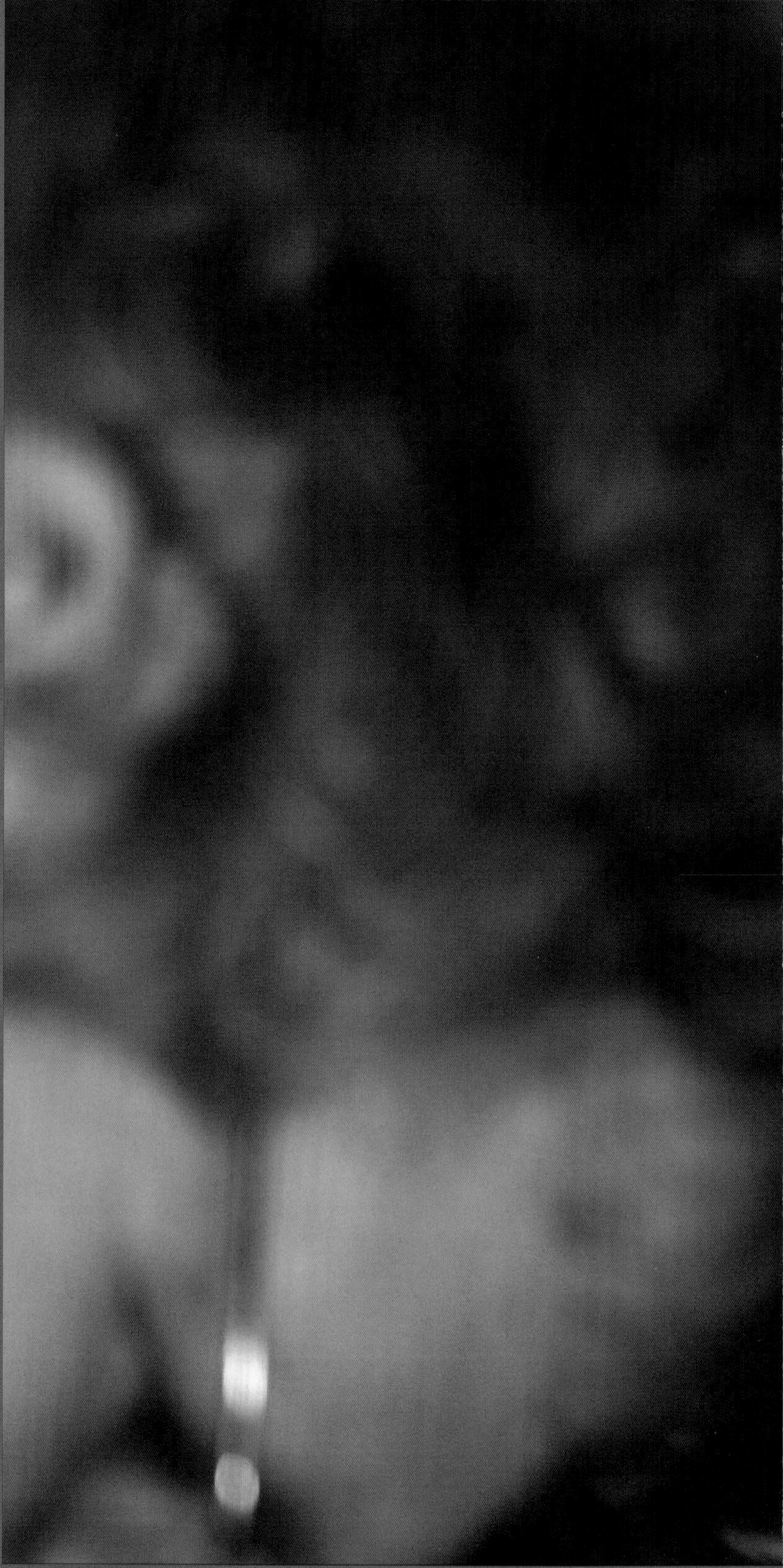

► In this digital age it's somehow reassuring to know that there's still a place in MotoGP for the old-fashioned combination of clipboard, pen and paper.

PAUL BARSHON

▲ Race face: Rossi stares into the distance as he and Jerry Burgess multi-task, juggling the variables of the complex equation linking suspension settings, chassis geometry, gear ratios, tyre compounds and lap times.
PAUL BARSHON

▲ The Brazilian GP divides paddock opinion. The under-30s just love going to Rio; the over-30s are usually too nervous to leave their hotel rooms.

PAUL BARSHON

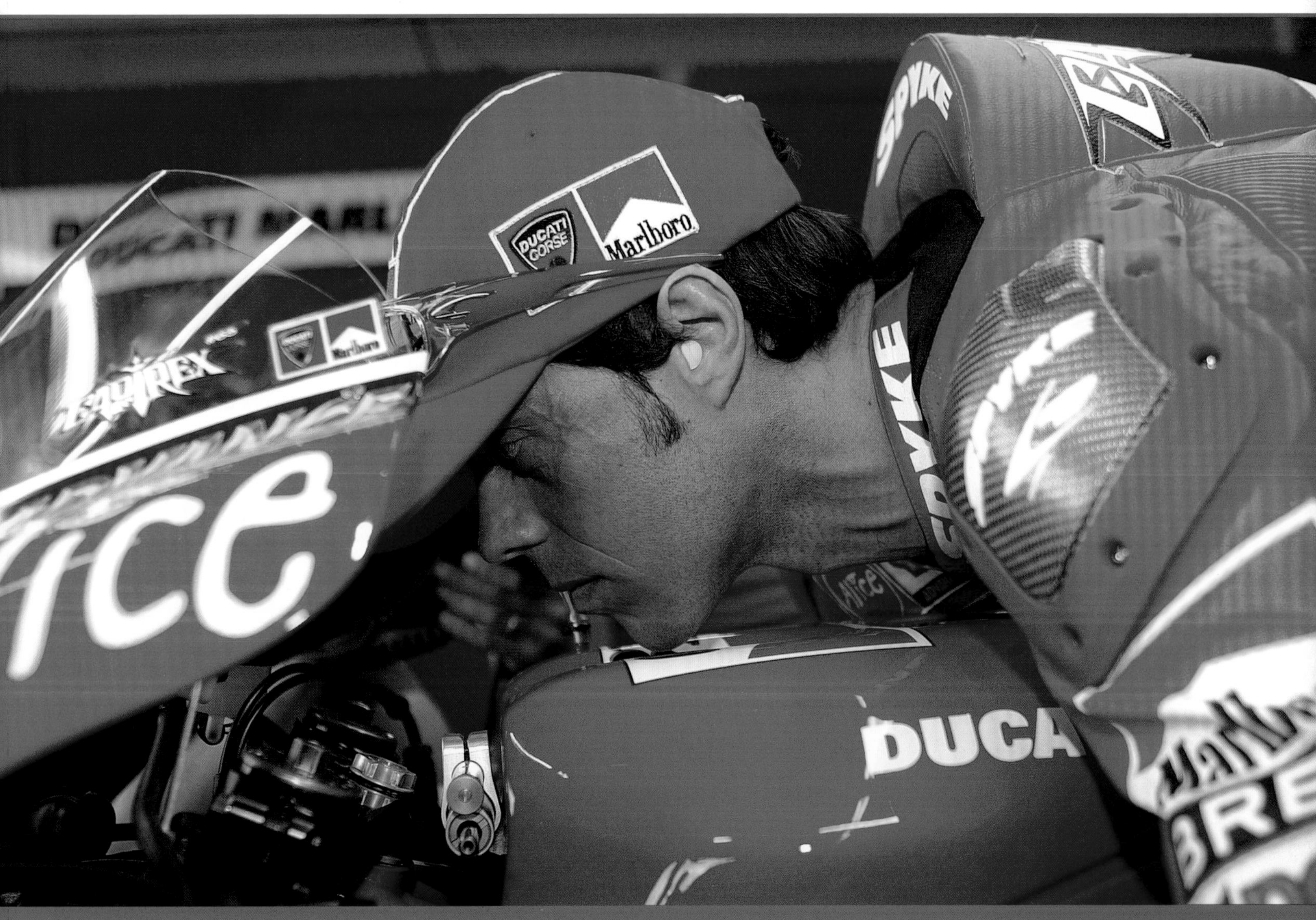

▲ Loris Capirossi tried hard to make the Ducati bend to his will but the 2004 model was a long way from being as competitive as the '03 bike.
HENK KEULEMANS

Arai
HELMET

◄Kenny Roberts, the 2000 World Champion, at last saw Team Suzuki's fortunes start to turn around. Pole position in Rio was the highlight of his year.
PAUL BARSHON

▲A switch to Bridgestone tyres seemed to suit the Suzuki. The factory also worked hard on improving the engine's electronic control system, which had caused Roberts and team mate Hopkins more than a few problems.
MARTIN HEATH

'The podium is good but I want to win races'

Nicky Hayden

You wouldn't get lighting like this during a race. This shot was taken late in the afternoon at the post-season Valencia test and shows Nicky Hayden, typically, still out there racking up the laps at 5.30pm.

PAUL BARSHON

◄ Trying to wrestle the Ducati Desmosedici into submission was such a tough job that it even reduced Loris Capirossi to despair; check the blisters on his hands.
MILAGRO

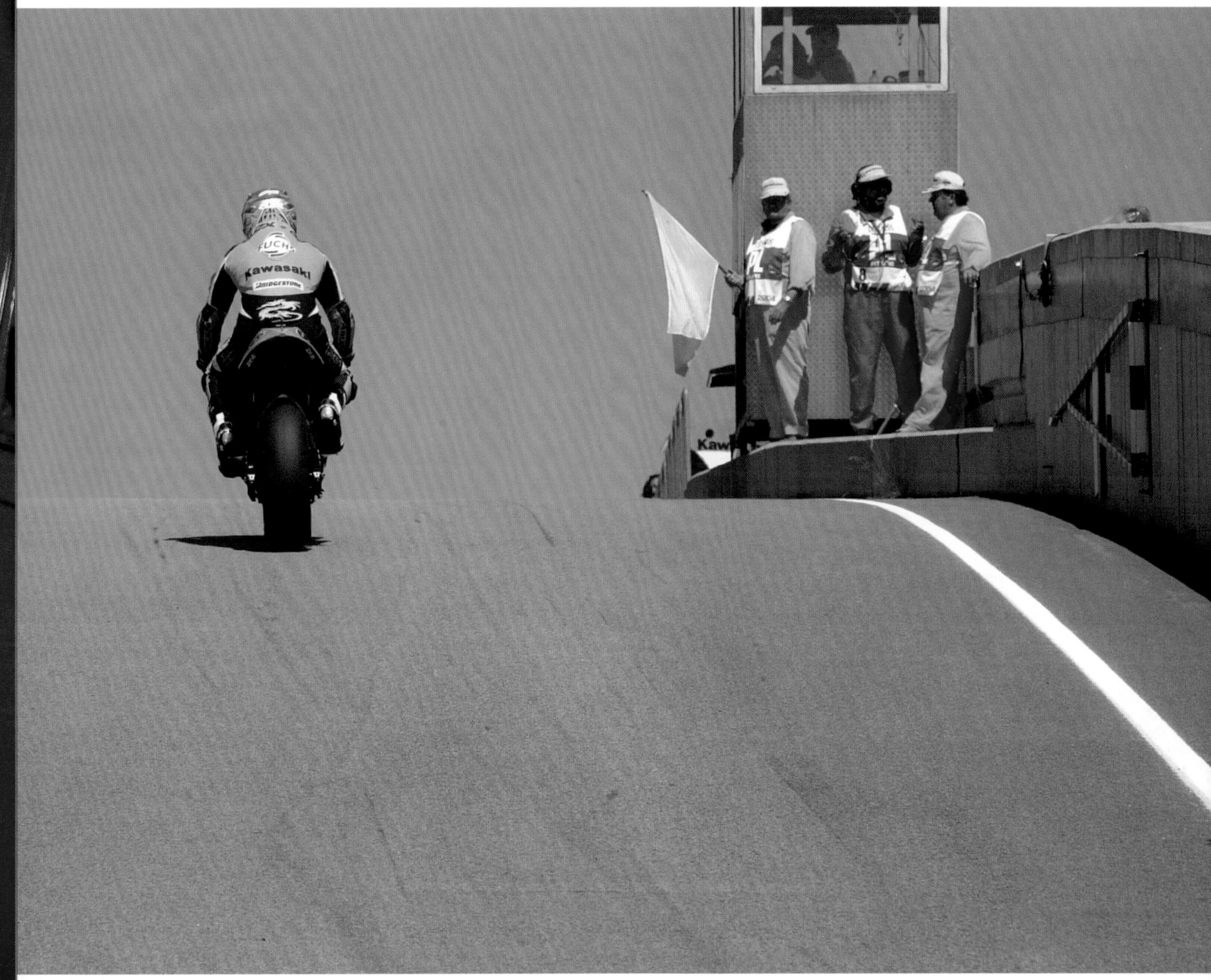

▲ Into the unknown: Alex Hofmann heads out of the Sachsenring pitlane to practise for his home GP. The horizon adds real drama to the image.
GERHARD RUDOLPH

agv
46
GAULOISES
GAULOISES
GAULOISES
YAMAHA
MOTUL

The story of the 2004 season: Valentino Rossi looks over his shoulder and sees Sete Gibernau in close pursuit. It had been much the same in 2003, but after the track-cleaning incident in Qatar the two could no longer be described as friends.
MILAGRO

movistar
movistar
movistar
33
Castrol
Castrol
SPIDI

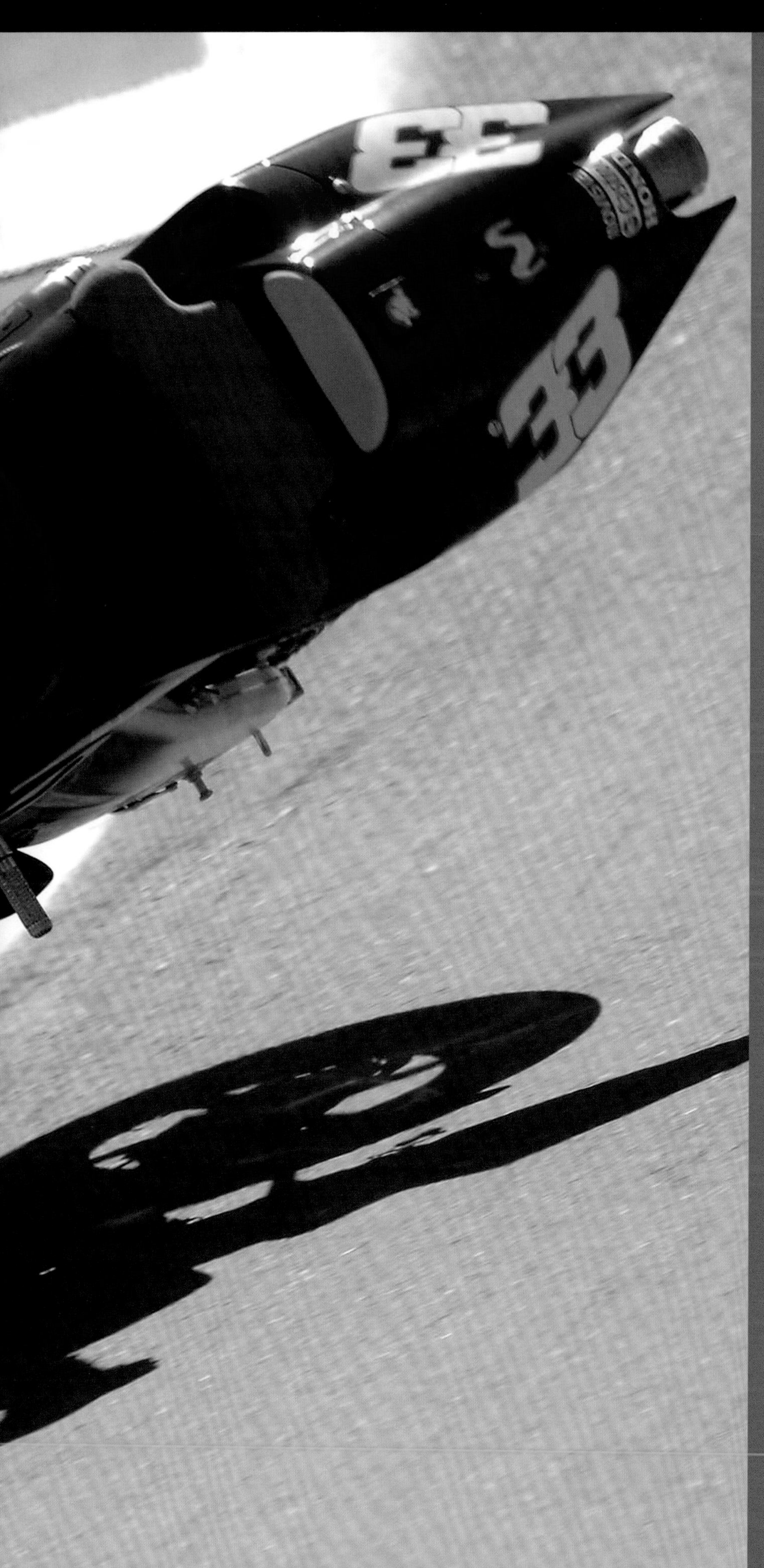

◀ When he first saw Laguna Seca, Marco Melandri decided he didn't like the track; in fact he said it was dangerous. It was a self-fulfilling prophecy, as he crashed three times, including in the race. This is his get-off at The Corkscrew during practice.
LUCASZ SWIDEREK

DANGER

Warning: motorsport can be dangerous – especially for the participants

There's no getting away from it: motorcycle racing isn't a sport you take up if your main ambition is to stay out of the hands of the medical profession. If a car racer gets a bit of oversteer he runs a little wide in the corner; if a bike racer loses the front he crashes. And even the mildest of crashes off a racing motorcycle is going to hurt. Often it hurts a lot. The punishment for a mistake on a racing motorcycle very rarely fits the crime.

The good news is that protective equipment has improved so much and circuits have become so much safer in recent years that really serious injuries have become a rarity. Minor damage, from bruising and abrasions to broken wrists and collarbones, is not. We've become so used to the sight of racers parting ▶

▼ 2004 was not a good year for Ducati. Their bike was nowhere near as rideable as the original model and the riders suffered accordingly. This is Loris Capirossi crashing out of third place in the German GP.
GOLD AND GOOSE

▶ company with their machines at three-figure speeds and walking away that it's easy to forget the risks involved. Nowadays a fallen rider doesn't hit an immovable object but no safety measure can prevent him tangling with his machine or other riders, as the terrifying five-man first-bend crash at the 2006 Catalan GP proved. Nevertheless, it's also possible to win a world title without crashing. Both Valentino Rossi and Sito Pons have become World Champions without falling off all season.

However, motorcycle racing still offers a bewildering number of ways to gain entry to Dr Costa's Clinica Mobile. Like most top-level sportsmen, MotoGP racers treat their bodies with worrying detachment, as another piece of machinery to be patched up and got back on track in the same way as a crashed bike, as quickly as possible. The first question after a crunching smash is always, 'How soon can I get back?' In that, at least, motorcycle racers are no different from any other professional sportsmen.

Very few racers are walking around without a limp, a few messy scars or some internal metalwork. That's the bottom line: racing is dangerous. It can be beautiful and it can be inspiring, but it can also be brutal and bloody. The Aussies got it right with the promotional slogan for their 2004 race: the posters promised 'Extremely Extreme Sport'.

▶ Capirossi bounces through Motegi's first-corner gravel trap after instigating the crash that also took John Hopkins, Kenny Roberts, Max Biaggi, Nicky Hayden and Colin Edwards out of the race. Note the massively padded gloves, a design evolved after numerous hand injuries.
GOLD & GOOSE

Marlboro
ADVANCE

'It really kicks in every gear, much more than my 500 ever did'

Regis Laconi

▶ This photograph, more than any other in this section, will cause any motorcyclist to wince. Other images in this chapter are more graphic, but this one captures that moment when you become horribly aware that you are in all probability going to be hurting a lot in the very near future. Remarkably, Regis Laconi stayed on after this moment at the 2002 French GP.
PAUL BARSHON

SHARK
aprilia
SECTOR
PlayStation 2
55
SECTOR
SECTOR
SPORT WATCHES
aprilia
DUNLOP

▲ Valentino Rossi assesses the situation after crashing in free practice for the 2006 Dutch TT. He damaged bones in his right wrist and ankle.

JEAN-AIGNAN MUSEAU

► The Dutch crash damaged Rossi's wrist enough to necessitate heavy strapping and pain-killing injections. 'I learn that preparing a wrist is like preparing a bike to race,' said Valentino of the precise timing and treatment necessary to get him fit to compete.

MARTIN HEATH

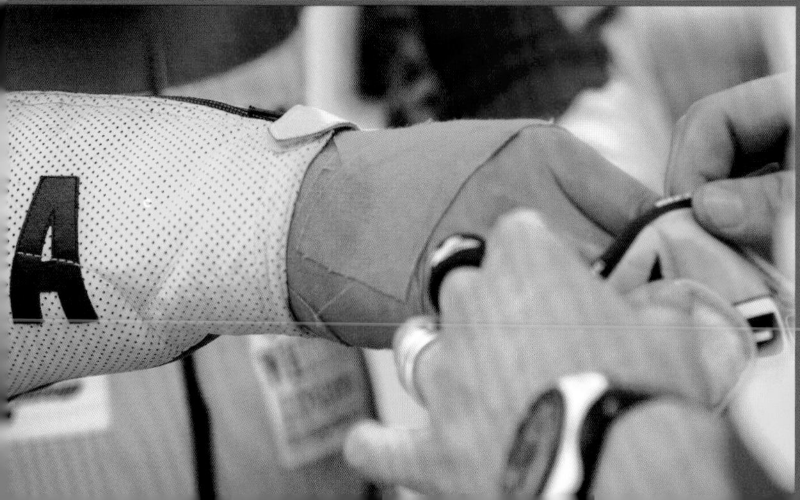

▲ Valentino walked away from this one, a massive crash in qualifying for Valencia, the final race of 2005. He lost the front at over 100mph and the bike had enough momentum to clear the trackside barrier.

GOLD AND GOOSE

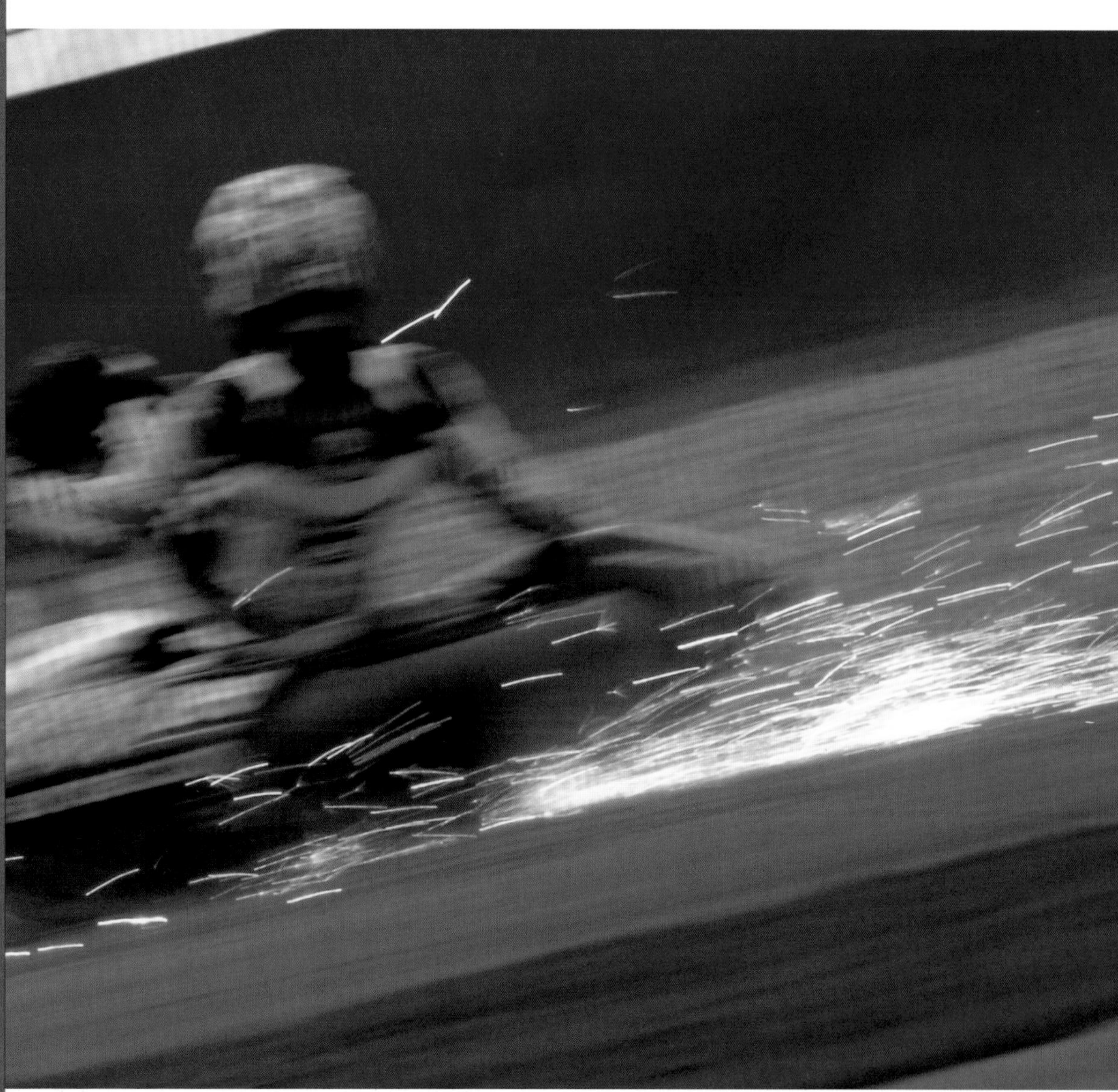

◄ Max Biaggi has just set the fastest lap of the 2003 German GP, making up for a bad start. He was closing the leaders down when he crashed on the fastest part of the circuit, the fast downhill two corners from home.
MILAGRO

▲ Casey Stoner hits the tarmac in a shower of sparks during qualifying at Shanghai in 2006.
MIRCO LAZZARI

▲ This famous sequence was the result of a loose filler cap at the 2003 German GP. The starting procedure for the Aprilia involved unscrewing the petrol tank filler cap and then retightening it once the motor was running. This time someone forgot to do it up again.

PAUL BARSHON

◄ Colin Edwards realises his Aprilia is a mobile inferno and bales out on the fastest part of the Sachsenring circuit. Thankfully, he escaped with superficial burns while the bike cartwheeled into the gravel trap at the bottom of the circuit.
PAUL BARSHON

The first corner of the 2006 Catalan GP saw the most destructive crash in the history of MotoGP. Sete Gibernau has already parted company with his Ducati after tagging team-mate Loris Capirossi (65), who is tangling with Marco Melandri (33). Dani Pedrosa (partially obscured) would also be brought down and Randy de Puniet (17) would be forced off track (see next page). Neither of the Ducati riders nor Melandri were able to make the restart.

SHIGEO KIBIKI

REPSOL
69
Fortuna
24
66
17
7
DUNLOP
10
Circuit de Catalunya
F
F
DANGER

▶ Start-line incidents are always scary and often injurious; there's nowhere to go if riders touch and no time to react if someone stalls in front of you. This is Welkom 2003 and Colin Edwards is on the floor after tangling with John Hopkins – note the smoke coming off his leathers.

MILAGRO

▼ Catalunya 2006, Turn 1, and the crash that shaped the season (see previous page for the start of this incident). Randy de Puniet, already in the gravel, is taking action to avoid Sete Gibernau's flying Ducati, which hit the tarmac at over 120mph.

LUCASZ SWIDEREK

► Tarmac scars on Max Biaggi's leathers tell you exactly how hard he hit the ground and how far he had to slide.
MILAGRO

No rider ever tried harder than Jeremy McWilliams. He made a career of forcing recalcitrant motorcycles to go faster than they wanted to. This time the Aprilia has refused to co-operate and Jeremy tumbles through a Sachsenring gravel trap.
GOLD AND GOOSE

▲ Kurtis Roberts has just realised that his dad's bike has caught fire after he crashed in practice for the 2005 Valencia GP. He rapidly got out of the way immediately after this picture was taken.

MARTIN HEATH

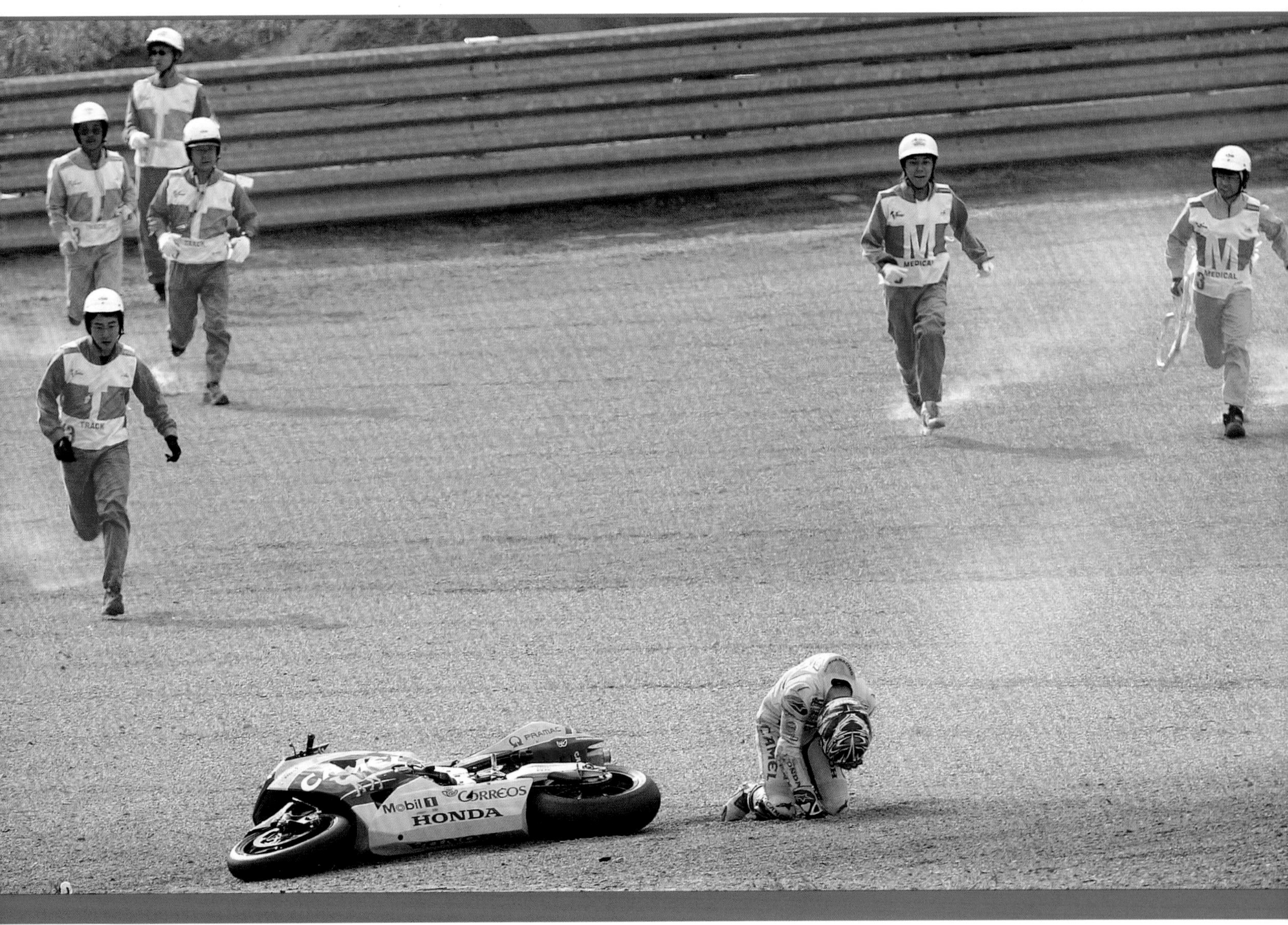

▲ A platoon of uniformly dressed and helmeted Japanese marshals rush to aid Tohru Ukawa, who has just crashed at the end of Motegi's back straight in practice for the 2003 Pacific GP.

ANDREW NORTHCOTT

'Fortunately I cannot remember the crash, I was asleep'

Marco Melandri

◀ Marco Melandri on the grid for the 2006 Dutch TT just six days after he had been involved in that massive crash at the Catalan GP. He finished seventh despite the damage you can see and an as yet undiscovered cracked collarbone.
ANDREW NORTHCOTT

▲ Donington Park is notoriously slippery in the wet. Marco Melandri finds out just how treacherous Goddard's – the final hairpin – can be in the 2005 British GP. He was just one of ten fallers.
MILAGRO

19
19
Kawasaki
Kawasaki
ÖHLINS
SRT

Sometimes crashing isn't just painful, it's embarrassing – such as when you take out your team-mate. At the 2005 German GP at Sachsenring, Olivier Jacque and Alex Hofmann managed to make it as far as the first corner.
ANDREW NORTHCOTT

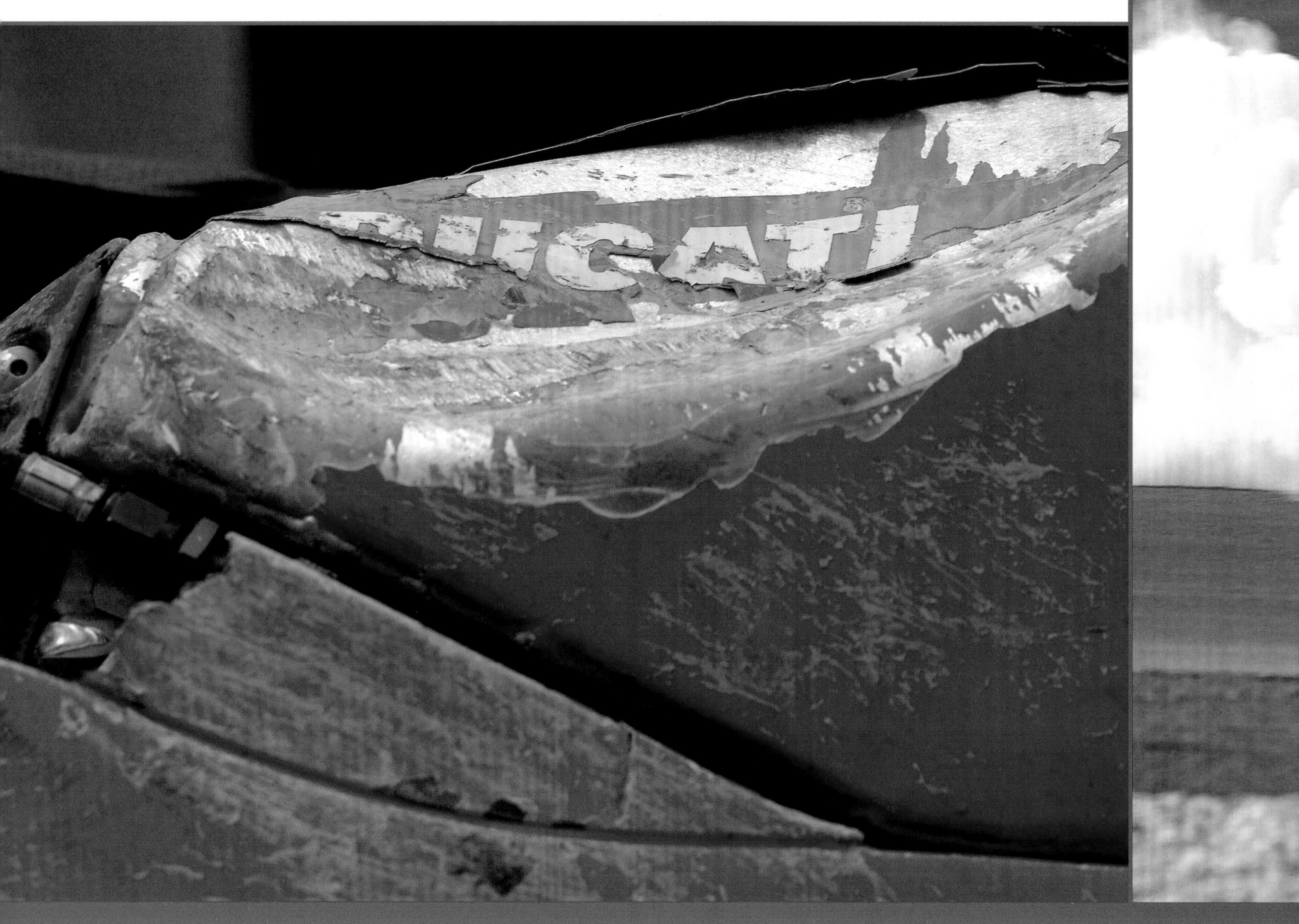

▲ The state of the Ducati's tank after the Barcelona 2006 crash tells you more than you really want to know about the forces involved.
MIRCO LAZZARI

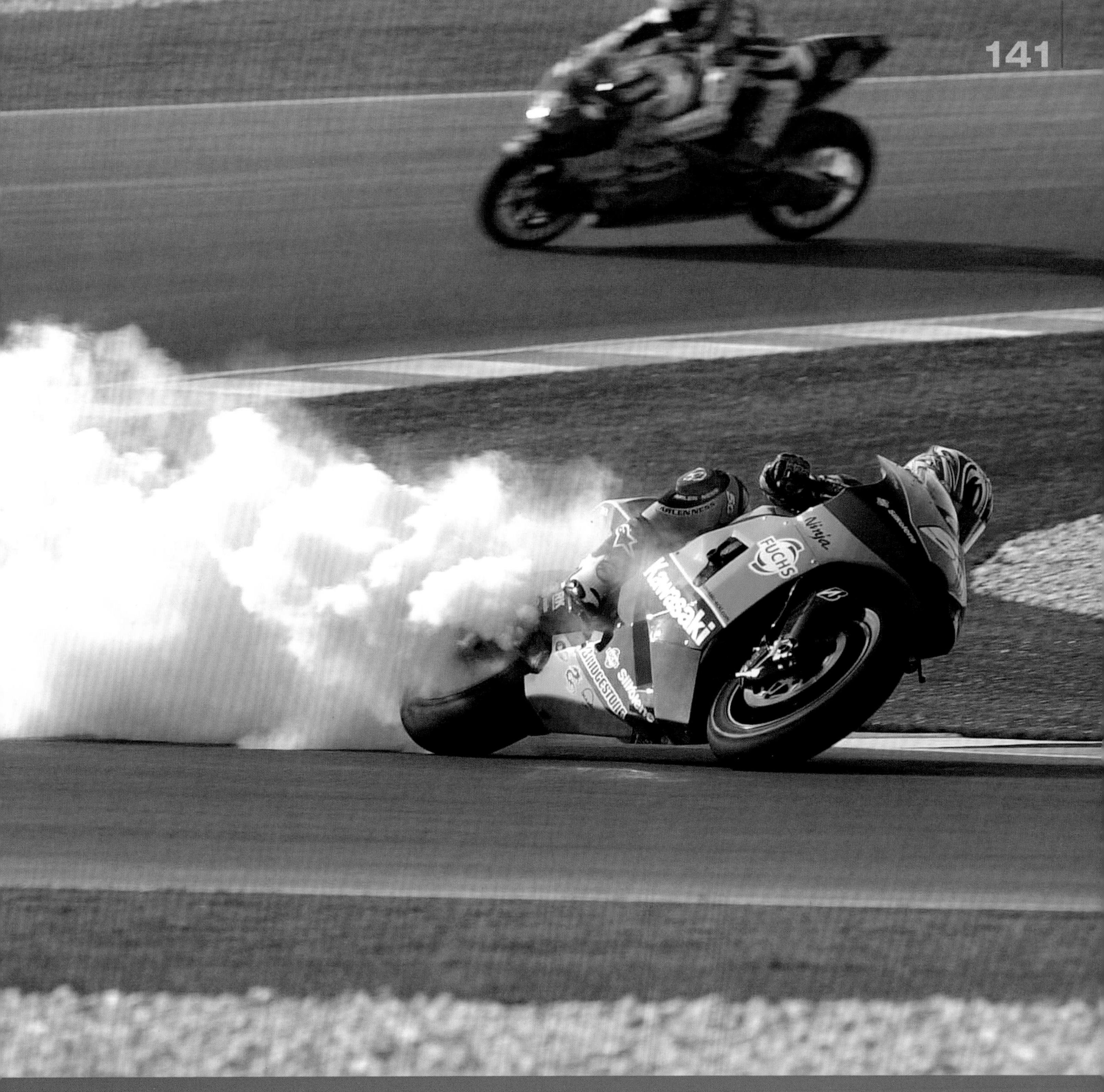

▲The most worried man in this picture is Alex Barros, on the Repsol Honda in the background. He's wondering how much oil has just been spread over the track by Shinya Nakano's terminally ill Kawasaki. The Japanese rider doesn't yet know what's going on.

PAUL BARSHON

spidi
NOLAN
Castrol
GAULOISES
YAMAHA
46

Valentino Rossi and Marco Melandri hit the Motegi tarmac at the 2005 Japanese GP. Rossi escaped unharmed while Melandri suffered a nasty wound. See that footrest? It's about to stab his right foot.
MILAGRO

movistar
15
Castrol
HONDA
Castrol
HONDA
BlackPrince
GAULOISES
46

◀The last corner of the first race defined the whole season. After Valentino Rossi had ridden a remarkable last lap, Sete Gibernau left a gap and the Italian went for it, the resultant coming-together sending the Spaniard on a trip through the gravel trap to second place, much to the displeasure of the Jerez crowd.
STAN PEREC

RACING
2005

Rossi the ruthless breaks yet more records

MotoGP came into focus after the upheavals of the previous three years. Sure, Valentino Rossi was still champion, but several other murky issues were cleared up.

On the technical side, every bike had a big-bang engine and a greater or lesser degree of 'fly-by-wire' throttle as electronics became the single most important tool of the designers and engineers. Ducati Corse pinpointed mid-year as the exact moment of this development, and it's unlikely to be a coincidence that this is when the red bikes started working in harmony with their new Bridgestone tyres. From Brno onwards, Loris Capirossi set pole three times in four races, scored back-to-back victories, got another podium ▶

and set a fastest lap. In Malaysia, the team got both riders on the podium for the first time. If Loris hadn't missed two races at the end of the season through injury, he could have been second in the championship. That honour went to Marco Melandri, despite three crashes in mid-season. After a fraught couple of years on Yamahas, he emerged as a genuine contender on the satellite team Honda. Over at the factory team, Repsol Honda replaced Alex Barros with Max Biaggi, only for Max to fail for the first time in his MotoGP/500cc career to win a single race in a season.

Nicky Hayden maintained his habit of starting the season slowly but then reeled off a series of firsts: first fastest lap, first pole position, first win. At the end of the season he rattled off four successive podium finishes, including a magnificent second to Rossi at Phillip Island. His fellow countryman Colin Edwards left Honda to be Rossi's team-mate and did exactly what he was employed to do: he was the only man to score points in every race of the year, helping Yamaha to the Constructors' Championship in their 50th year.

The man who didn't figure in the battle for second place at season's end was Sete Gibernau. The hex that Rossi had put on him after the Qatar race of 2004 seemed to work: Sete didn't win another race. He should have done. First he was the victim of a brutal Rossi move on the last lap of the first race of the year – Gibernau left a gap and Valentino forced his Yamaha into it. Sete then crashed in two races while leading, ran off track while leading in three more, and suffered two mechanical failures and two more crashes. For two seasons, Sete had been the only man able to challenge Rossi week in, week out. Perhaps a merely great rider can only maintain that level of intensity in the face of genius for a given period of time before it all becomes too much.

On the technical front, fuel-tank capacity was reduced from 24 to 22 litres, and it was decided that in 2007 the capacity limit for MotoGP engines would be reduced to 800cc.

Rossi carried all before him yet again, and he did it in some new countries. MotoGP made an overdue return to the USA and went to the shiny new Formula 1 facilities in China and Turkey. Other riders shone, sometimes they even won, but no-one came close to doing what Gibernau had done for the past two seasons – challenge Rossi over the length of a season. More records fell: Rossi won more races in a season than any Yamaha rider ever.

Any arguments about Rossi's greatness resolved into whether he or Mike Hailwood was the best ever. That is, of course, a debate that can never be won. The difference between motorcycle racing now and then is so great that meaningful comparisons are impossible. What is beyond argument is that Rossi is the greatest motorcycle racer of the modern era. The mere fact that he won this title on a Yamaha as easily as he had won on a Honda is the best proof of that.

◄Sete Gibernau leads the pack through the first two corners at the Catalan GP. He led for over half the race but Rossi went to the front with three laps to go and pulled away; it was the pattern of much of the season.

ANDREW NORTHCOTT

▲The WCM team built their own bike and went Grand Prix racing with James Ellison as their rider.

GOLD AND GOOSE

2005 TIMELINE

10 APRIL
For the fifth successive season, Valentino Rossi wins the opening race of the year after colliding with Sete Gibernau at the final corner.

1 MAY
Valentino Rossi wins the first GP of China. It's his first wet-weather win for Yamaha. Olivier Jacque gives Kawasaki their best ever MotoGP result with second place.

4 JUNE
During practice for the Italian GP the MSMA confirms that the capacity limit for MotoGP will be reduced to 800cc for 2007, along with a further 1-litre reduction in fuel tank capacity.

25 JUNE
The last race on the classic 3.7-mile Assen circuit sees Rossi become the first Yamaha rider to win the Dutch TT twice and the first to win five GPs in a row.

10 JULY
MotoGP returns to the USA. Home favourite Nicky Hayden wins his first MotoGP race.

◄Marco Melandri finished the year a convincing second in the championship despite having three non-scoring races due to crashes. His last four races of the year saw him push Rossi all the way in Qatar, set his first fastest lap in Australia, and then win in Turkey and Valencia, setting the fastest lap in both. They were his first wins in MotoGP.
GOLD AND GOOSE

▼The Bridgestone-Ducati combination came good in the second half of the year. From Brno onwards Loris Capirossi took pole three times in a row, won two in a row, and set a fastest lap. It was by far the best run in Ducati's short MotoGP history and it would have been even better but for a massive practice crash at Phillip Island that put him out of two races.
ANDREW NORTHCOTT

31 JULY
German GP: Valentino Rossi wins his 50th premier-class race in 150 starts and equals Mike Hailwood's record of 76 wins in all classes.

25 SEPTEMBER
Malaysian GP: Loris Capirossi sets pole position and wins two races in a row for the first time (he'd won in Motegi seven days previously). These are the first back-to-back wins for Ducati and Bridgestone. Second place was good enough for Rossi to retain his title.

1 OCTOBER
Qatari GP: Rossi takes his tenth win of the year, the first time a Yamaha rider has ever won that many races in a season.

23 OCTOBER
Marco Melandri wins the first ever Turkish GP. It's also his first win in MotoGP.
He backs it up seven days later by winning at Valencia.

▼Olivier Jacque replaced the injured Alex Hofmann for MotoGP's first visit to China and promptly scored second place, his and Kawasaki's best ever result in the class.
ANDREW NORTHCOTT

►Toni Elias joined MotoGP, riding for Yamaha's second team, but suffered a nasty testing crash after Le Mans. Always spectacular to watch, he had a storming end to the season and attracted the attention of the Gresini Honda team for 2006.
ANDREW NORTHCOTT

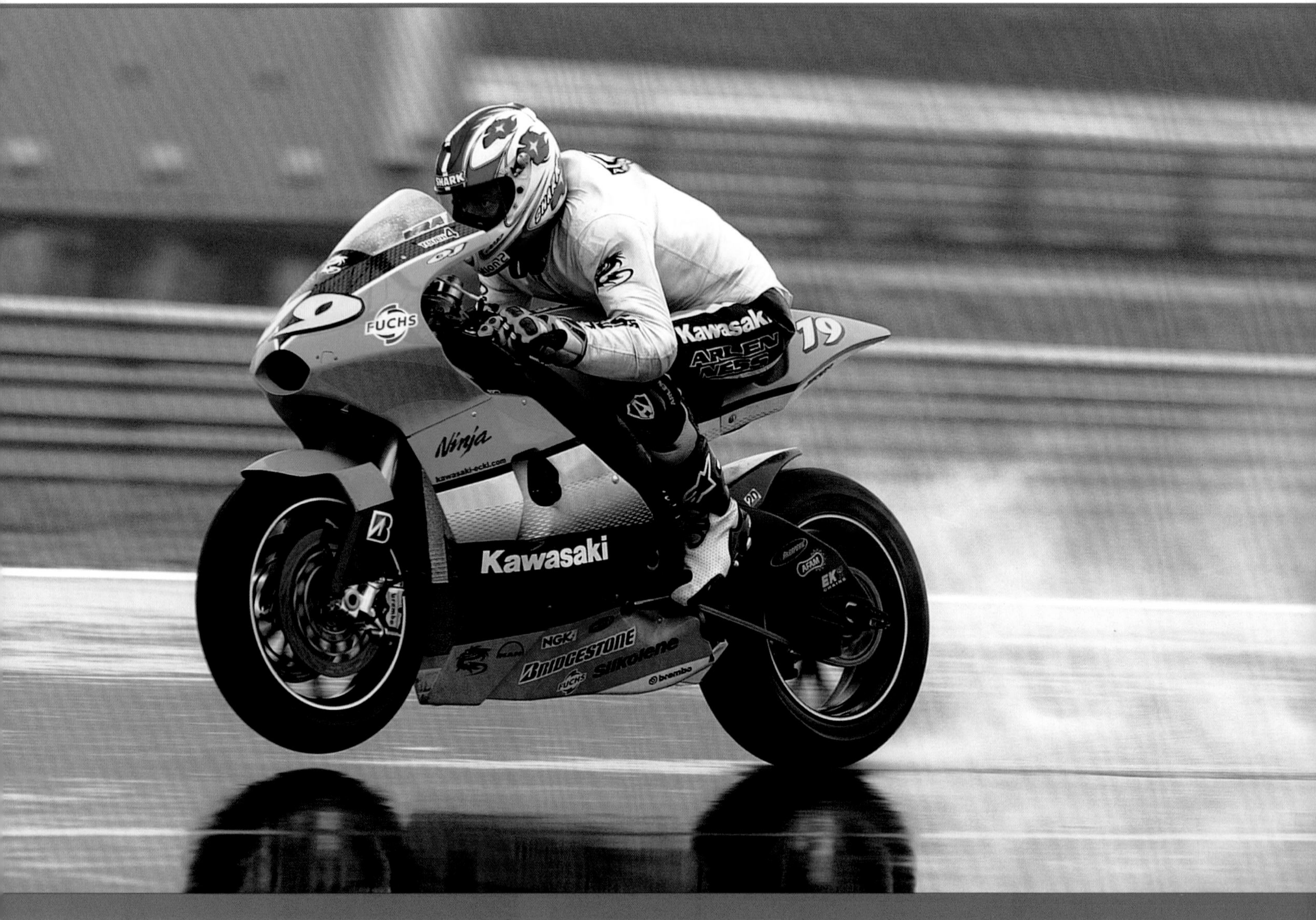

'At first I felt like a hair in the soup, now I feel like a fish in water'

Olivier Jacque

Fortuna
X-lite
X-801R
MOTUL
www.ToniElias.com
Fortuna

The British GP was held in truly awful conditions and produced one of the great rides from Valentino Rossi. This is the first corner; the reflection of the safety car's lights on the streaming track adds a weird dimension to the image, reminiscent of a 1970s Space Invaders game.

ANDREW NORTHCOTT

▼At the Sachsenring Valentino Rossi drew level with Mike Hailwood's record of 76 wins in all Grand Prix classes. 'It is always disappointing when someone arrives at your level, so I decide to apologise.'

GOLD AND GOOSE

►Repsol mechanic's note to self after the Dutch TT as the paddock packed the flight cases for the trip to Laguna Seca and GP motorcycle racing's return to the USA.

GOLD AND GOOSE

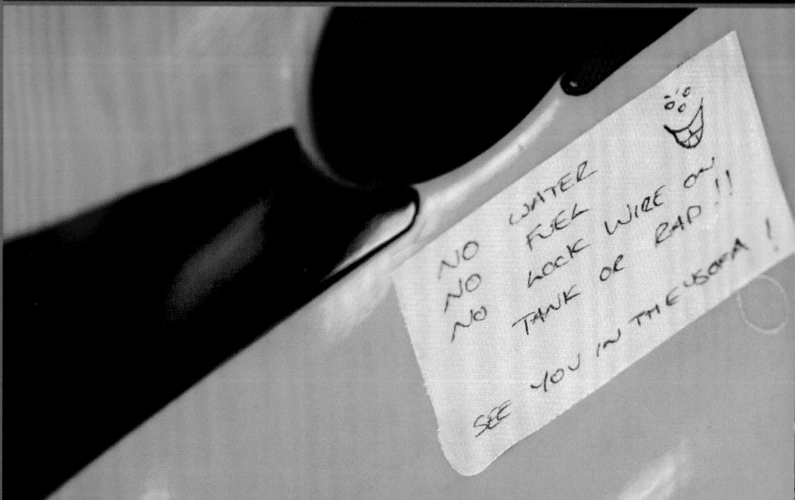

▲ Sometimes it all goes right for a photographer. Shooting down through the trees at the Sachsenring is a standard trick but this time Patrick Lundin managed to frame Kenny Roberts' crash helmet and the Suzuki's tank in a gap in the foliage.
GOLD AND GOOSE

Sete Gibernau's challenge as Rossi's only real rival finally ran out of steam after two years. He suffered appalling luck in the races but was by far the best qualifier of the year with 14 front-row starts – including five pole positions – in 17 races.
ANDREW NORTHCOTT

◀Local hero Nicky Hayden trounced the opposition at home at Laguna Seca for his first win in MotoGP. To make it a perfect day for the home crowd, there was an American one-two with Colin Edwards in second place. The happy return to the USA was slightly overshadowed by worries about safety, but improvements were promised for 2006.
ANDREW NORTHCOTT

▲To help celebrate their 50th anniversary, Yamaha brought along their past champions, including Agostini, Lawson and Rainey, and sent the team out in the American importer's colours made famous by Kenny Roberts Senior.
GOLD AND GOOSE

REGINA
PROTON
riders
MICHELIN

◀ Jeremy McWilliams made a one-off appearance on the old Roberts V5 at Brno after the team fell out terminally with KTM. The Austrian company supplied Team Roberts with engines for the first half of the season.
ANDREW NORTHCOTT

▲ Max Biaggi, Sete Gibernau and Colin Edwards indulge in a little formation flying at the Sachsenring.
MILAGRO

The unmistakable style of John Hopkins on the Suzuki. Hopper again showed his raw talent but had a tendency to make mistakes when there was a chance of a rostrum finish – notably in Portugal, China and the UK. Back-to-back front-row starts towards the end of the season hinted at better things to come.
ANDREW NORTHCOTT

SUZUKI
MOTOGP
SUZUKI
MOTUL

11
Fortuna
66
65
6
KONICA MINOLTA
SHOEI
PRAMAC
DUNLOP

◀ The pack plunge down the Corkscrew at Laguna Seca. TV cameras tend to flatten out the scenery but this angle shows you that it must feel like riding off the edge of a cliff.
LUCASZ SWIDEREK

▲ Rossi and the chequered flag: a well-conceived camera angle and a bit of luck produce a pleasing effect.
ANDREW NORTHCOTT

Yamaha went back to their corporate red-and-white colour scheme for the final race of the year at Valencia as part of their 50th birthday celebrations. Valentino Rossi felt it necessary to add a cartoon crash helmet design to top things off.
MILAGRO

YAMAHA
agv
1
TRIBÙ DEI CHIHUAHUA
DOCTOR
YAMAHA
YAMAHA

◀ There's no doubt who the outside world recognises as the face of MotoGP – even when he's hidden in the shadows.

MILAGRO

FACES

The movers and shakers of MotoGP – so that's what they look like

It would be instructive to work out what percentage of the photographs taken by the professionals who cover MotoGP are portraits. It must be high. Not that it's hard to work out why – nothing interests people as much as other people.

There's always something to be read into an expression. Top MotoGP racers, like any prominent people, from film stars to politicians, tend to assume a public face as a way of protecting themselves from the constant attention. Which means that a picture of them with their guard down can be both fascinating and revealing. The face of a winning Valentino Rossi, for instance, is very different from the one you see when he has been beaten and the jester's mask slips. ▶

▶ Suguru Kanazawa, President of HRC, picked up the pieces after Rossi left Honda and then oversaw Nicky Hayden's championship campaign of 2006. In typical Honda corporate style, his next career move was to Swindon to manage the company's car plant.

MILAGRO

▶ And that face, of course, is all the more interesting because it's rarely seen.

Then there's the matter of putting faces to names. Journalists and TV commentators rattle off the names of all manner of paddock people from team managers and engineers to race officials and sponsors, but unless you're a regular at the races you wouldn't know them if you sat next to them on a bus.

It's especially important for the world outside the MotoGP paddock – or any other top category of motorsport for that matter – to see the racers without their crash helmets, otherwise they're mere automatons, anonymous machines. That's why there are those ten minutes after the sighting lap and before the warm-up lap when riders sit on the grid, to let the TV cameras show the viewers at home what they really look like. No sportsman is going to become a household name without becoming a household face.

Anyone who has taken an interest in MotoGP for even a brief period of time will no doubt be able to recognise all the riders on the grid. What you might not be able to do is put faces to some of the other names you've seen and heard. This chapter will introduce you to some of those people – team managers, engineers, officials – who you might not otherwise have recognised but who have all played important parts in the development of MotoGP.

▲ There are always cameras in your face when you're Valentino Rossi, so you might as well play up to them from time to time.

MILAGRO

GAS
HRC
MotoGP

▶ Shinya Nakano rode Yamahas for the first two years of MotoGP but from 2004 to 2006 he spearheaded Kawasaki's effort. In the first year he took the marque's first front row start and scored their first rostrum in the top class since 1981, but only one more rostrum followed in the next two years.
GOLD AND GOOSE

▲ Ichiro Yoda came to Kawasaki from Yamaha in 2005 with 15 years of Grand Prix experience behind him, including the role of development engineer on the original M1 project. As technical director, he oversaw Kawasaki's move from screamer-engined 'super-superbike' to competitiveness with a big-bang engine and Bridgestone tyres.
ANDREW NORTHCOTT

▲Max Biaggi never minded being the centre of media attention, provided it was on his terms.

PAUL BARSHON

◄Race Direction out on patrol: on the left is Rider Safety Delegate Franco Uncini, the 1982 500cc World Champion, and on the right the Race Director, Paul Butler.

GOLD AND GOOSE

▶ Managing Director of Yamaha Racing Lin Jarvis, the man who brought Valentino Rossi to Yamaha.

GOLD AND GOOSE

▲Bob MacLean and Peter Clifford, team principals of WCM, won 500cc GPs as Red Bull Yamaha (but then lost their sponsor), became the last team to run a 500cc two-stroke, and then built their own four-stroke. The bike started life on Clifford's kitchen table and was good enough to score points.

GERHARD RUDOLPH

◄Takeo Fukui started with Honda in 1969, was chief engineer of Honda R&D during the NR500 project, became chief engineer and then president of HRC, went back to Honda Motor Company as chief of motorcycle development, then had a spell in the USA. Now he's President & CEO of the entire Honda Motor Company, but still finds time to come to the races.

ANDREW NORTHCOTT

▶ Politics on the pit wall. Dorna CEO Carmelo Ezpeleta and Sito Pons, then President of IRTA, deep in conversation.
GERHARD RUDOLPH

▼ Kenny Roberts Snr was a champion as a rider and team owner, and now he's a constructor. The King is always ready with a cheery greeting for passing photographers.
FRIEDEMANN KIRN

Marlboro
ADVANCE
MICHELIN
FILA
DUCATI
Marlboro

◀ Claudio Domenicali, CEO of Ducati Corse, and his technical director Filippo Preziosi study the pit timing monitors. The racing company employs just 115 people out of the 1,000-plus who work for Ducati – numbers that are much smaller than those of the big four Japanese companies.
GERHARD RUDOLPH

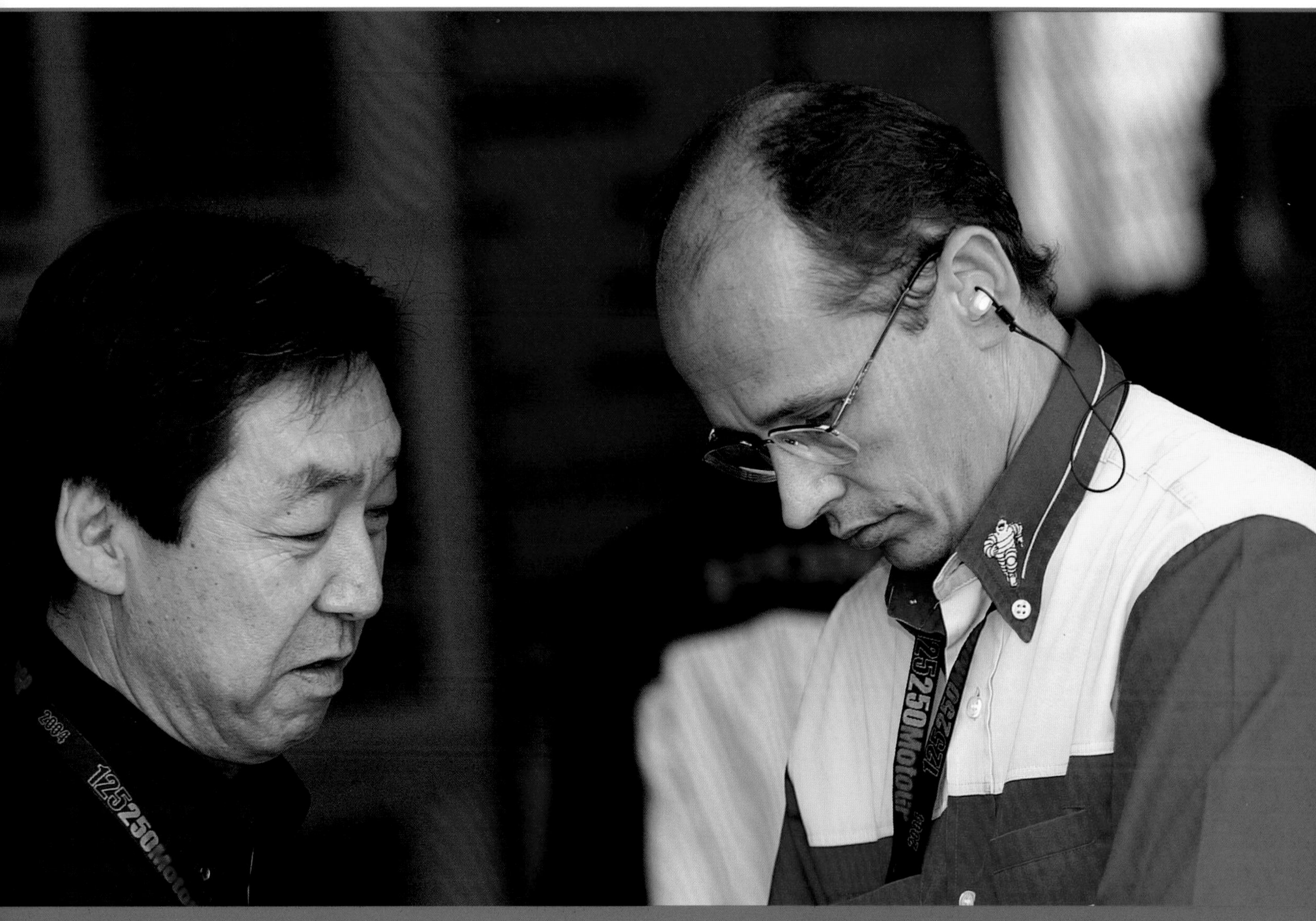

▲ HRC Managing Director Satoru Horiike with Nicholas Goubert of Michelin. Horiike-san joined Honda in 1978, was chassis designer on the NR500 and NSR500, and project leader on the RC45. Goubert was Michelin's chief of motorcycle competition for the whole of the 990cc MotoGP formula.
HENK KEULEMANS

▼ Paul Denning took over the running of the factory Suzuki team from long-time manager Garry Taylor in 2005. The team runs out of Denning's family business, Crescent Suzuki, in the South of England.

GOLD AND GOOSE

▼Livio Suppo, Ducati's team manager arrived in MotoGP via rallying and the Benetton Honda 125 team that very nearly took Marco Melandri to a world title.

GOLD AND GOOSE

◀Garry Taylor was Suzuki team manager for over 20 years before handing over to Paul Denning. He was instrumental in the development of the four-stroke GSV-R project. Garry (right) is seen here discussing tactics with Stuart Shenton, John Hopkins's race engineer, prior to the 2004 Czech Grand Prix.

GOLD AND GOOSE

▶ It can be thirsty work – Sete Gibernau cools off after a hard day at the office.

MIRCO LAZZARI

▼ Team Roberts' 2005 flirtation with KTM as their engine supplier lasted just over half a season. The fall-out, when it came, was terminal – as can be gauged from the expressions of Team KR's Chuck Aksland and KTM's Kurt Nicoll.

ANDREW NORTHCOTT

► A bit of reflected light picks out Jerry Burgess in the Yamaha team's pit counter. The Australian has been race engineer to Valentino Rossi since he arrived in the top class and has been responsible – along with Yamaha's Maseo Furusawa, manager of the specially formed Technology Development Division – for turning the M1 from also-ran to the equal of the Honda.
GOLD AND GOOSE

HONDA
GAS
HONDA
69
REPSOL

◄ Nicky Hayden shows how to attack the left-hander over the blind crest before the last corner at Valencia – one of the trickiest stretches of tarmac in MotoGP. He finished third in this race and became World Champion.
ANDREW NORTHCOTT

RACING 2006

Nicky Hayden overcomes the odds to become the last 990cc World Champion

Nothing much was supposed to change in the final year of the 990s, but it did. For once the Yamaha/Rossi/Burgess axis got it wrong. Despite exemplary results in pre-season testing, when the racing started they found they had a bike that chattered terminally when it had a lot of grip. More often than not, this ruined Rossi's qualifying and put him in the middle of the pack, forcing him into high-risk moves in the first few corners. Some said Rossi had bad luck, but it might be more correct to say he put himself in riskier positions than he was used to.

The first corner of the first race set the pattern: a collision with Toni Elias put Vale on the floor. Then there was tyre failure in China, engine failure in France, injury in Holland, another engine failure in the USA, and finally ►

a crash in Valencia. With that litany of woe, it's truly amazing that he was able to claw back a deficit of over 50 points to Nicky Hayden during the second half of the season and go into the final round of the year as the points leader.

Hayden also struggled against the odds. Honda required him, and him alone, to ride the development machine known within HRC as the Ghost Bike. This gave the impression of being a rolling prototype for the following season's 800cc formula. Other makers, notably Suzuki and Kawasaki, were also using the season in this way. The Kenny Roberts team found an unexpected lifeline to stay on the grid – thrown by Honda. After a career spent fighting against HRC, Kenny Senior was offered Honda engines. He didn't refuse and Kenny Junior took two rostrums and four front-row starts. When he finished third at Catalunya he was ten seconds behind the winner, and in Portugal he should have won.

In the factory team, Hayden was working on his own with a motorcycle that was notably slower than most of the opposition. However, his new-found aggression was a reminder that he'd grown-up in the rough and ready school of US dirt-track racing. In previous years he'd often dropped back through the field once he'd been passed. But when Rossi passed him in Qatar, Nicky repassed immediately. At Assen he sent Colin Edwards up a slip road and in Germany he was willing to put his body on the line to prevent his team-mate passing.

Hayden's team-mate was Dani Pedrosa, who, along with fellow rookies Casey Stoner and Chris Vermeulen, joined forces with only slightly more experienced youngsters like Toni Elias to rock the established stars. After Stoner's pole in Qatar, Rossi opined that he 'rides like he's been in the class ten years'. In China Pedrosa became the first rookie winner in the top class since the great Freddie Spencer, while Vermeulen took pole in Turkey and got on the rostrum in Australia. It was the year of the youngster, although Pedrosa's methodical approach contrasted wonderfully with the flat-out-from-the-word-go technique of Stoner.

It was also a year of shocks. Two races from the end of the season it looked as if Hayden was cruising to the title. True, he'd seen his points lead eroded, but he appeared calm and in control. Then came Estoril and a desperate overtaking manoeuvre early in the race by team-mate Pedrosa, of all people, put both men on the floor. As if that wasn't enough, Elias then rode the race of his life – mainly sideways on the rumble strips – to snatch victory and a vital five points from Rossi. And so it went down to the wire at the final race under the 990cc formula, and the shocks kept coming.

Troy Bayliss turned up at Ducati as a replacement and reminded us why he'd been on the Desmosedici when it first appeared. It was the only win by a wild-card or replacement rider in MotoGP. In the race, we witnessed not one but two of that rarest of specimens – a Rossi mistake. Valentino made a hash of the start then crashed in a slow corner. Hayden stayed calm and rode to third – and the title – behind the two Ducatis. What we didn't know was that he was carrying a nasty shoulder injury from that Portuguese crash.

Rossi was generous and fulsome in his praise of the new champion, saying he admired the way Nicky conducted himself off the bike as much as his riding. Nicky felt good about it too: 'I didn't just beat the kid down the block...'

◀ Troy Bayliss rocked up to the last race of the 990cc era and blew the championship regulars away. He became the first man to win a World Superbike race and a MotoGP race in the same season, and the oldest winner in the top class since 1977. Here he sits on the stool he always brings on the grid before a race, exuding all the attitude of a boxer about to answer the bell for the decisive round.

ANDREW NORTHCOTT

▲ Valentino Rossi's Yamaha rolled to a halt at Le Mans while he was leading the race comfortably. The body language was eloquent; two DNFs in succession meant a deficit to Nicky Hayden of 40 points after just five rounds. Retaining his title would be a virtual impossibility and he knew it.

GARETH HARFORD

2006 TIMELINE

26 MARCH
Spanish GP: Loris Capirossi wins and leads the championship for the first time. Dani Pedrosa finishes second and becomes the first rookie since Biaggi and Haga at Suzuka in 1998 to finish on the rostrum in his first race.

8 APRIL
Qatari GP: Class rookie Casey Stoner starts from pole in just his second MotoGP race.

30 APRIL
Turkish GP: Nicky Hayden finishes third in his 50th MotoGP race and goes to the top of the points table for the first time. Casey Stoner's second place makes him the youngest Australian rider to stand on the podium for a race in the top class of GPs.

14 MAY
Chinese GP: Dani Pedrosa takes his maiden win in only his fourth MotoGP race. He becomes the joint second-youngest winner of a top-class race and the youngest rider to win in all three classes of GP racing.

4 JUNE
Italian GP: Rossi takes his fifth consecutive victory at Mugello and becomes the second most successful 500cc/MotoGP rider of all time.

18 JUNE
Catalan GP: Kenny Roberts' third place is the first ever rostrum finish for his father's team.

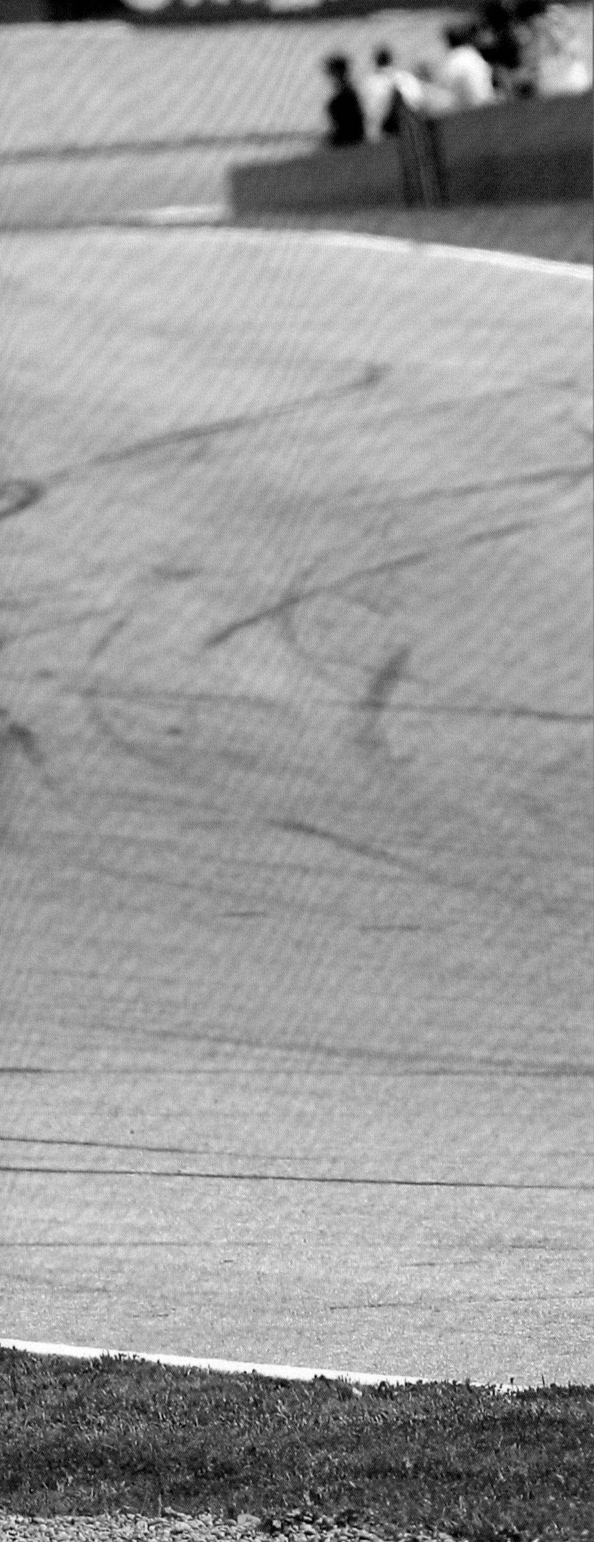

◀ Valentino Rossi watches the field disappear after a coming together with Toni Elias put him on the floor at the very first corner of the year. Moments later he was picking his bike up and chasing them, but it was the first of a succession of crashes and mechanical failures that dogged his attempt to win the final title of the 990cc era.

SHIGEO KIBIKI

▼ Casey Stoner led the wave of new young talent that threatened to overwhelm the MotoGP old guard: pole position in his second race and a rostrum in his third shocked the opposition.

ANDREW NORTHCOTT

24 JUNE
Dutch TT: Nicky Hayden gives Honda their 200th win in the 500cc/

20 AUGUST
Czech GP: Loris Capirossi's win 16 years and 15 days after his first GP victory (the 1990 British 125cc race) makes his the

17 SEPTEMBER
Australian GP: The flag-to-flag wet-weather rules are used for the first time; every rider pits to change bikes. Marco Melandri

23 SEPTEMBER
The MSMA announces new tyre regulations for the 2007 season, limiting riders to using 31 tyres during a race weekend.

15 OCTOBER
Portuguese GP: Toni Elias takes his first MotoGP victory in one of the most dramatic motorcycle

29 OCTOBER
Valencia GP: The final race of the 990cc era is won by Troy Bayliss, who becomes the first wild-card or replacement rider to win a MotoGP race. Capirossi is second to give Ducati their first ever one-two, and Hayden is third to become the

Dani Pedrosa leads his team-mate Nicky Hayden onto the home straight at Shanghai. They traded lap records before the Spaniard took his first MotoGP victory in just his fourth race in the top class.

ANDREW NORTHCOTT

NOLAN
Spain's Nº1
HONDA
domino
33
Spain's Nº1
Castrol
Castrol
HONDA
Spain's Nº1
Spain's Nº1
HONDA
valsir
castrol
HONDA

◀ Marco Melandri flies under the Dunlop Bridge at Donington Park tucked in behind the fairing, leaning the bike right to get back across the track ready to brake for Foggy's Esses – and he has both tyres clear of the ground. This is the fastest part of the circuit – Marco is doing nearly 170mph.

JEAN-AIGNAN MUSEAU

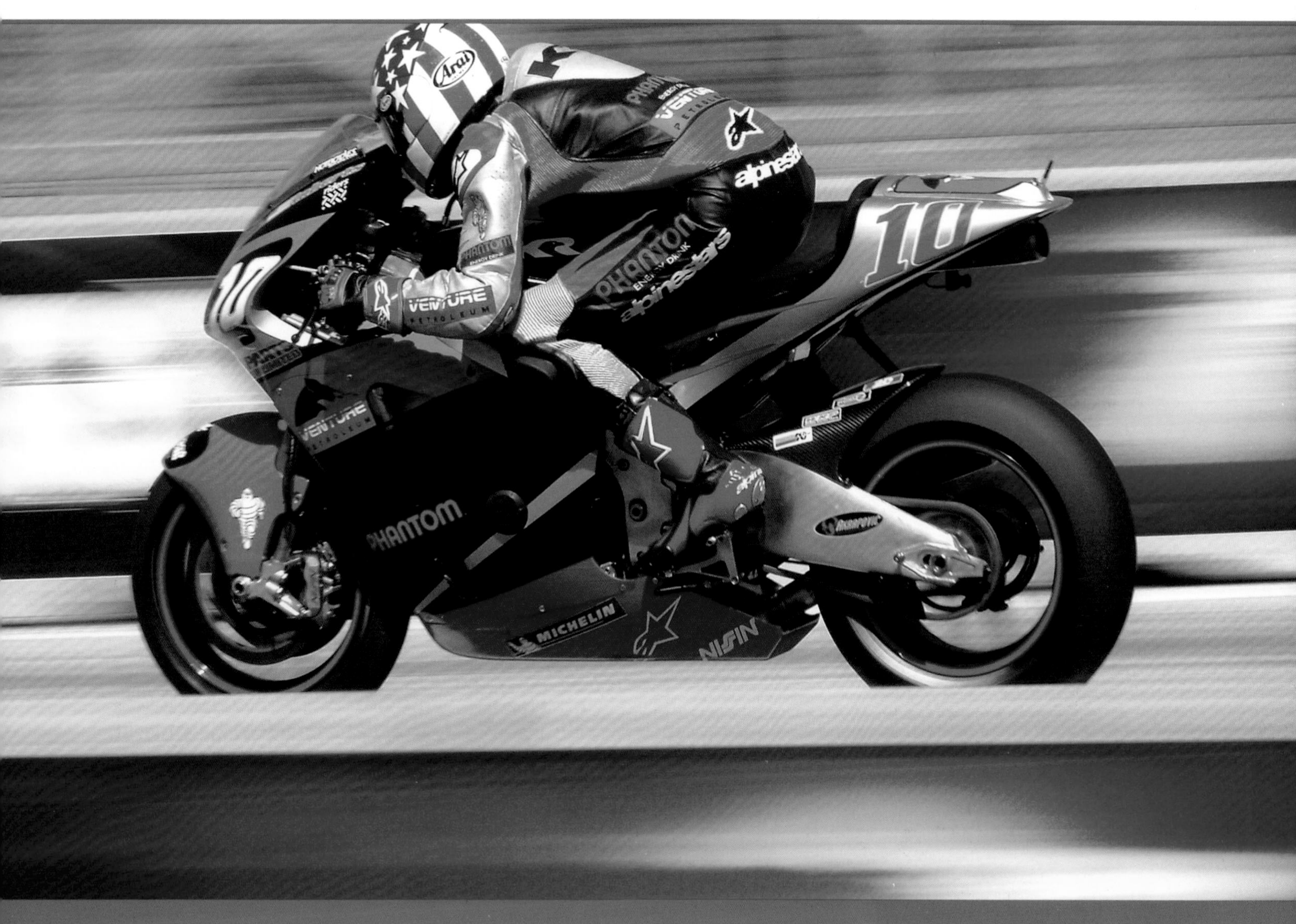

▲ Kenny Roberts on his way to fourth place in the USA. The bike's livery was part of the plot of a film being made with MotoGP as part of the backdrop; the helmet design was either a tribute to Peter Fonda in *Easy Rider* or a patriotic one-off for his home race.

MIRCO LAZZARI

The field files round the Omega at the bottom of the hill in first gear early in the first lap at the Sachsenring. The next right-hander is seven corners away – the blind fourth-gear turn that leads to the fastest part of the circuit.

MIRCO LAZZARI

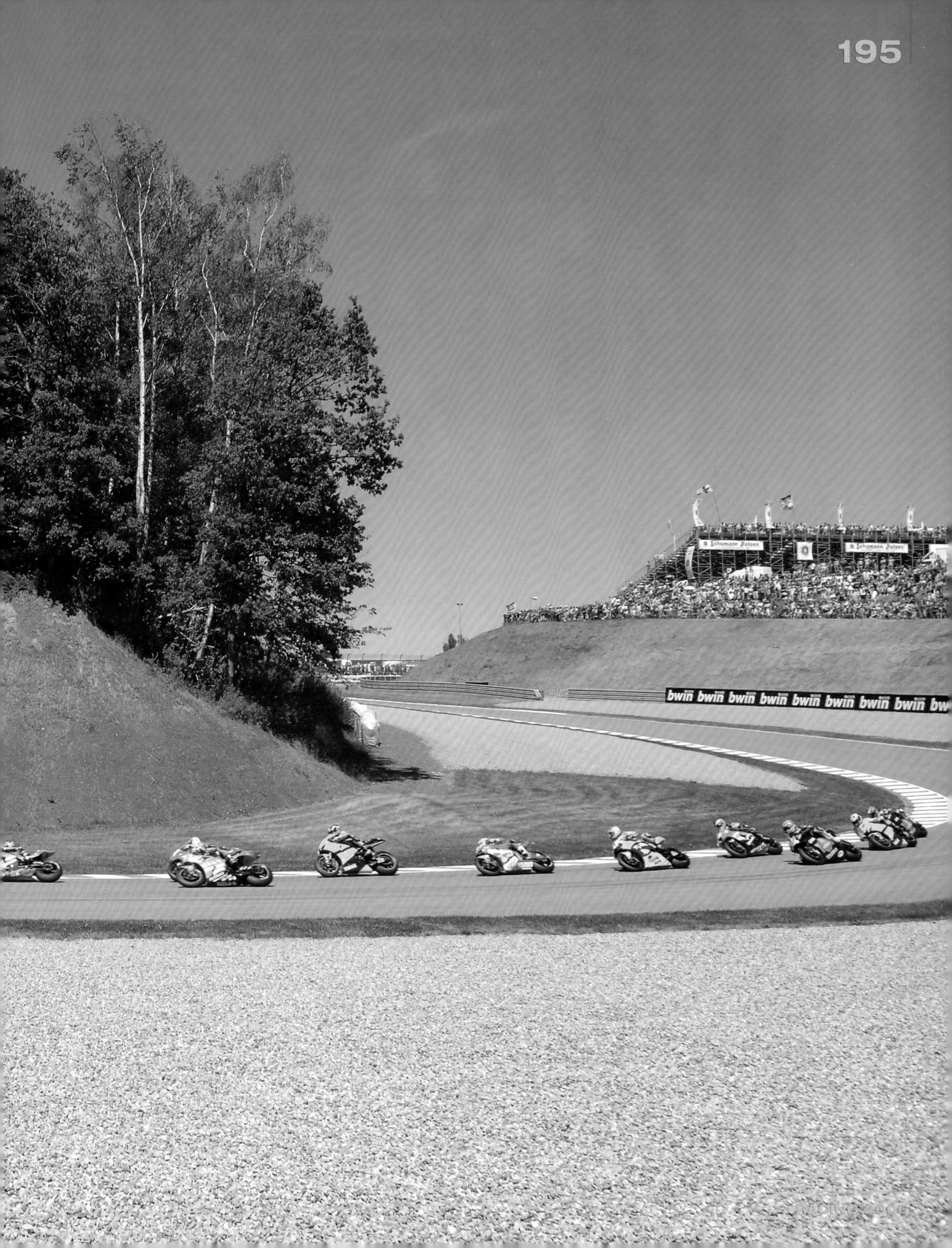
bwin bwin bwin bwin bwin bwin bwin bwin bwin

◀ It could only be Mugello. Shinya Nakano gets a wonderful view of some stunning Tuscan countryside.

GARETH HARFORD

◀ Colin Edwards and Nicky Hayden go into the final chicane at the Dutch TT. Both made mistakes going in, but Hayden stayed on his wheels and went on to win his first race outside the USA. Edwards fell when he ran on the Astroturf that edges the track but remounted to finish 13th.

ANDREW NORTHCOTT

▲ No doubt who was the unluckiest man of 2006 – Loris Capirossi. He was only 23 points behind Hayden at the end of the year despite his Catalunya crash putting him out of that race and severely handicapping him in the next four.

ANDREW NORTHCOTT

▼ Photographers don't like Qatar very much. The Losail International Raceway is absolutely flat and featureless, making it difficult to produce an interesting image. Shooting through a gap in the Armco barrier is one alternative...
LUCASZ SWIDEREK

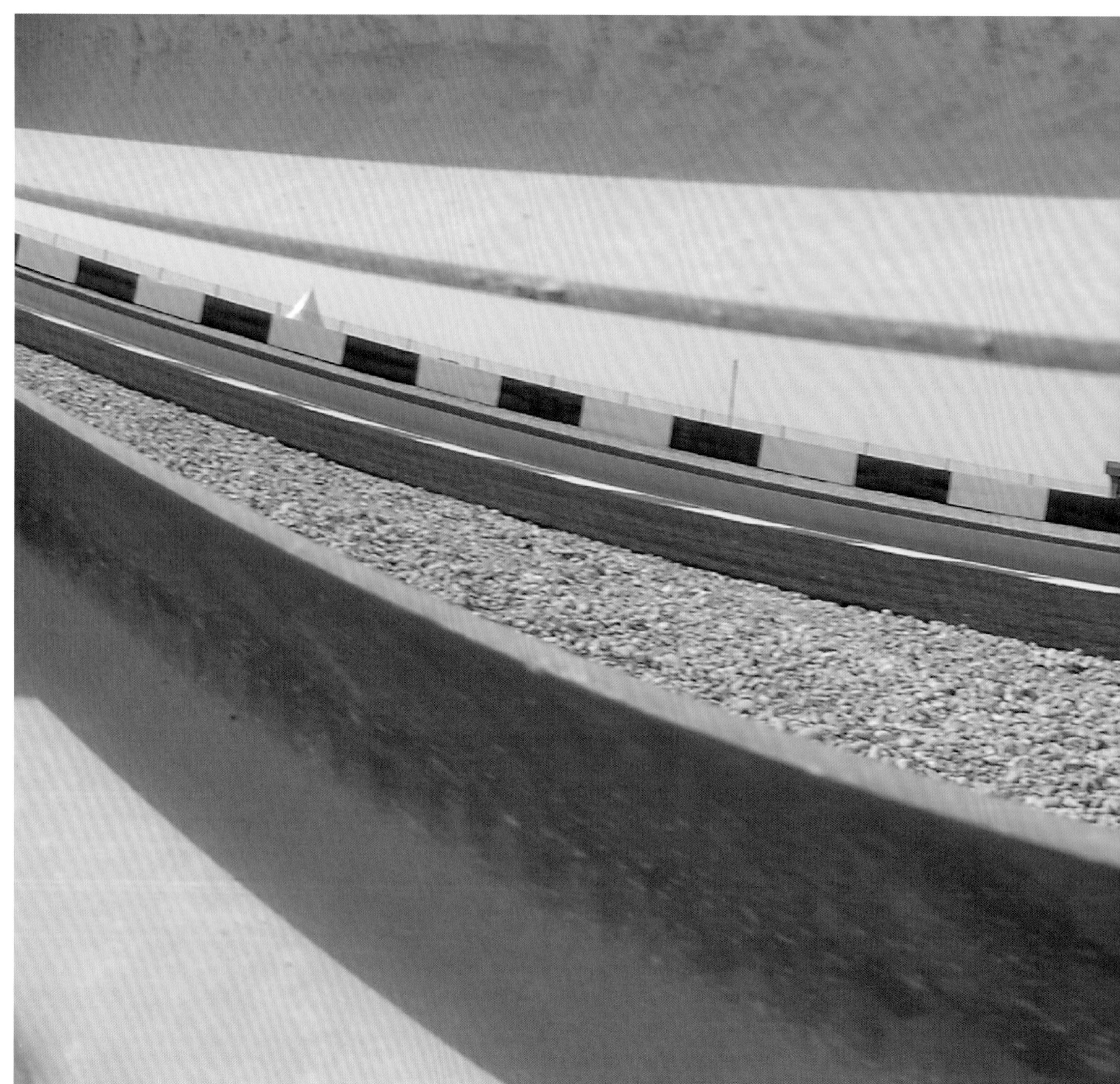

'Valentino Rossi is probably the best we've ever seen'

Mick Doohan

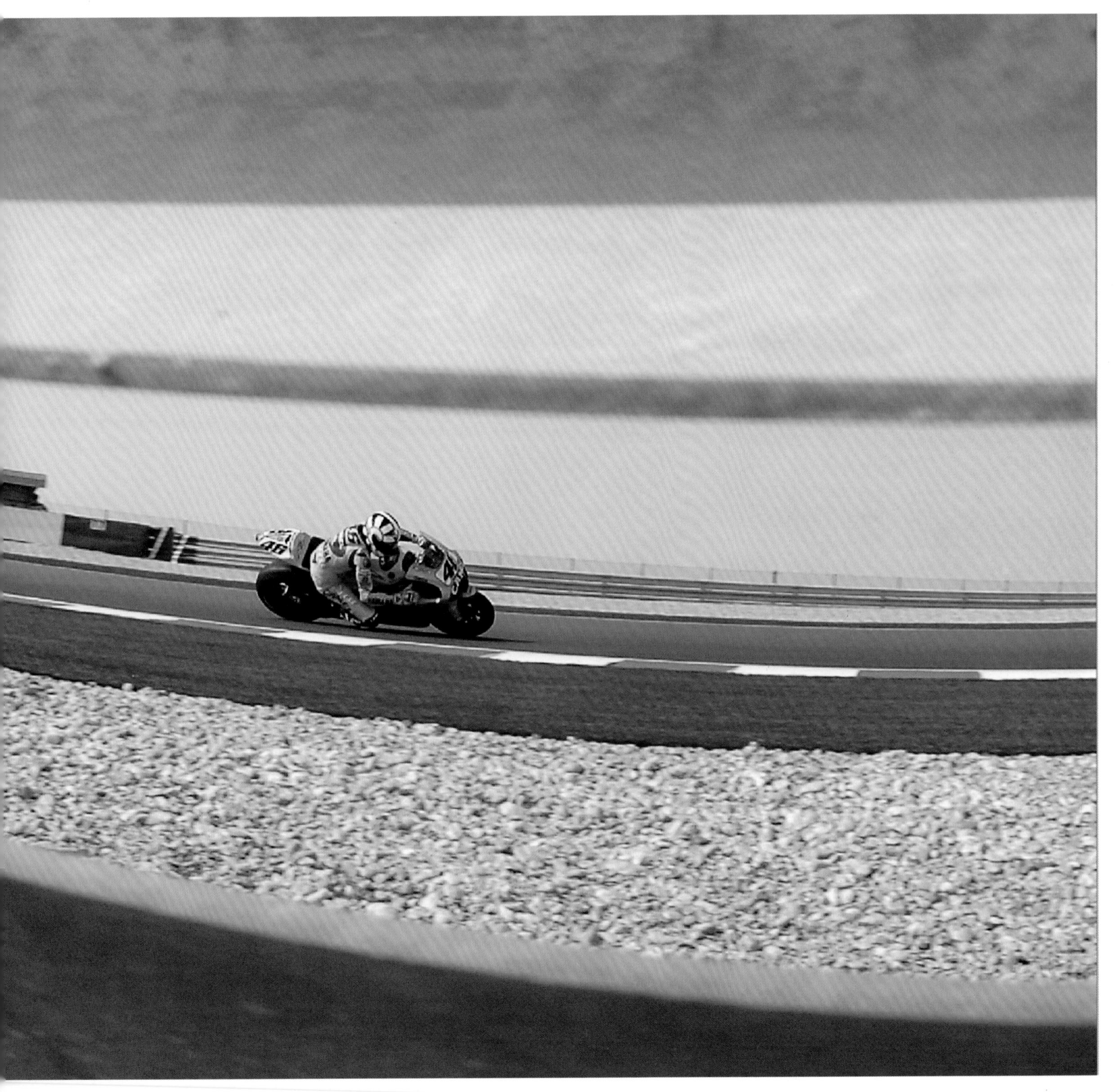

▸ John Hopkins got Suzuki's first dry-weather MotoGP pole at Assen but was overshadowed by new team-mate Chris Vermeulen most of the season.
ANDREW NORTHCOTT

▴ Chris Vermeulen was another impressive rookie. The Aussie arrived via the World Supersport and Superbike Championships and took the Rizla Suzuki team's first pole position and rostrum in Turkey and Australia respectively. However, his best race was in the USA where he scored a dry-weather pole and was robbed of a rostrum – at least – by fuel vaporisation problems in the heat.
ANDREW NORTHCOTT

RIZLA+
alpinestars

▲ Nicky Hayden and Valentino Rossi on the grid in pole and second place for the Malaysian GP. By now Hayden's big lead in the title trail was being rapidly eroded race by race, mainly by Rossi.

MILAGRO

▶ One of the best photos of 2006 – Sete Gibernau in practice for the Chinese GP demonstrating the efficiency of Bridgestone's wet-weather rubber and Ducati's traction control.

ANDREW NORTHCOTT

agv
THE DOCTOR
YAMAHA
46
TEAM
dainese
TEAM
dainese

If it rains in qualifying but not in the race, then all the photos taken on Saturday are very unlikely to be used by any newspaper, magazine or website. This image is from qualifying in Istanbul; it would be a shame to waste it.
LUCASZ SWIDEREK

▼Nicky Hayden flat-out through the pine forests of the Czech Republic during the lonely defence of his championship lead.
GARETH HARFORD

▼ Nicky falls to his knees during his slow-down lap at Valencia after winning the world title. The fact that the photographer has shot into the sun has added to the obvious emotion of the occasion.
MIRCO LAZZARI

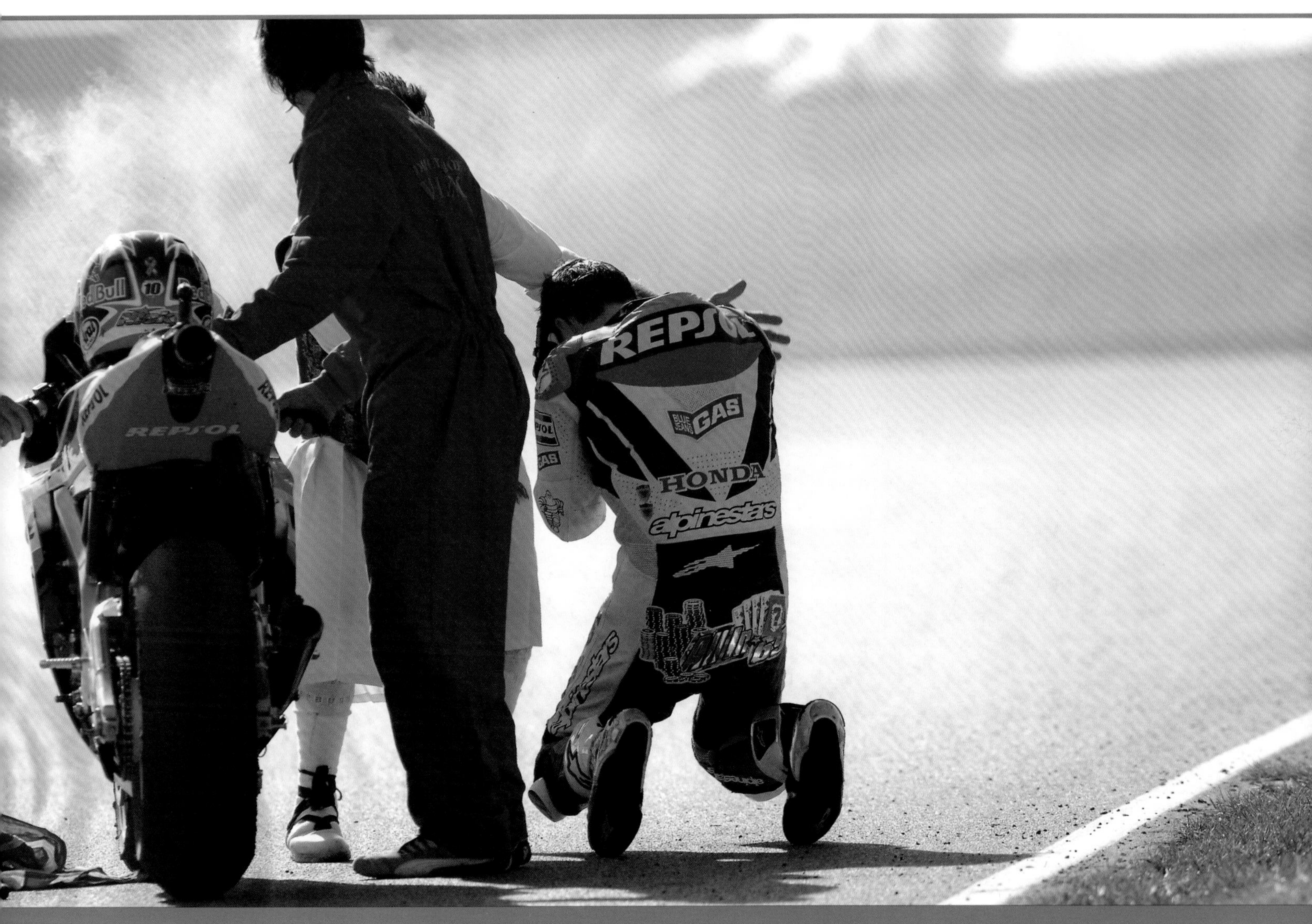

'We have never seen a better season of racing'

Kenny Roberts Snr

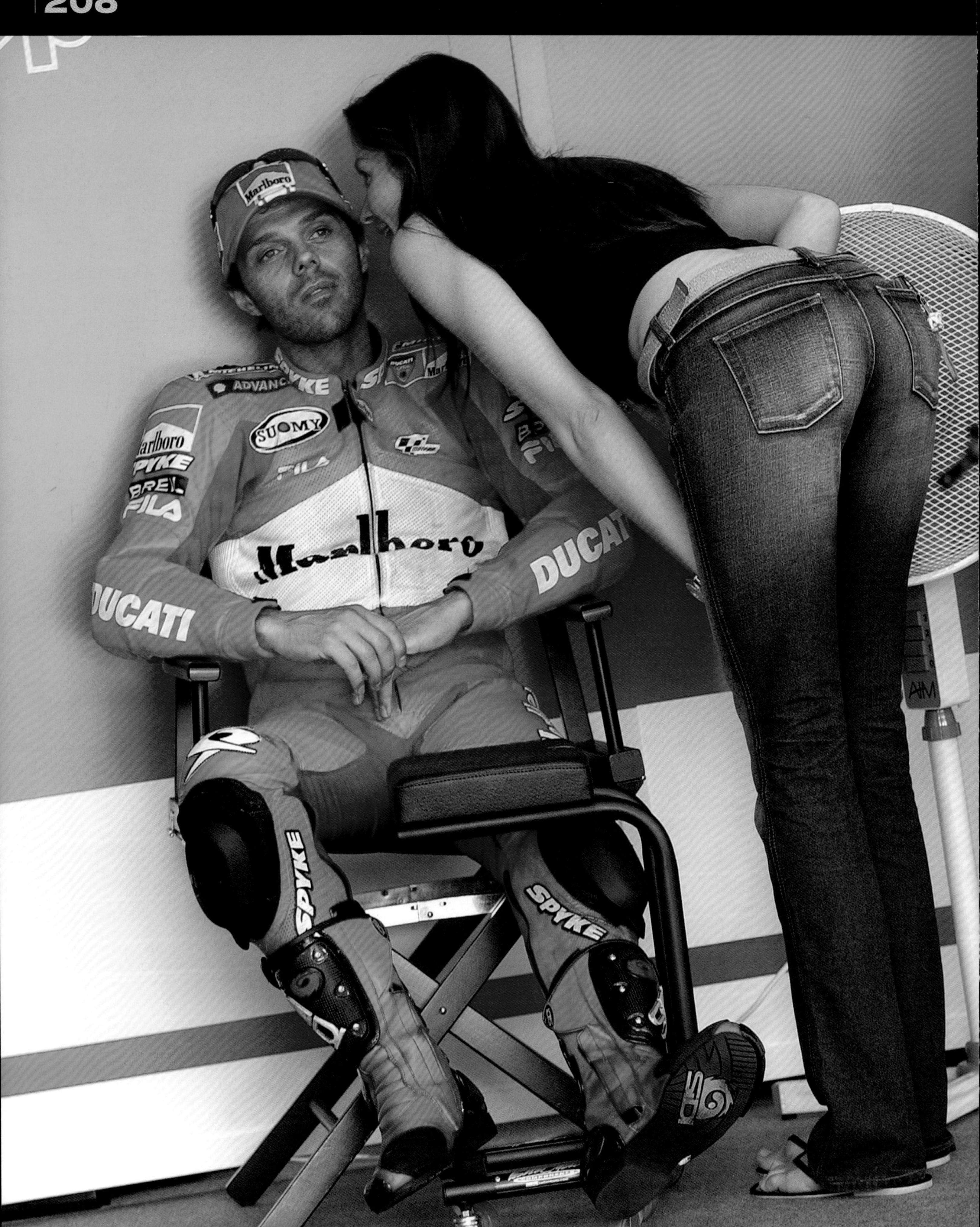
Marlboro
ADVANCE
SPYKE
SUOMY
FILA
BREIL
DUCATI
SPYKE
SIDI

◄ A study in domestic contentment: Mr and Mrs Capirossi discuss what pasta Ingrid will be cooking once Loris gets back from work.
PAUL BARSHON

PADDOCK LIFE

It's better than having a real job

The MotoGP paddock is like a medium-sized village of a couple of thousand people that happens to pull up its roots and move location every two weeks. The core of the population remains constant – riders, mechanics, media people, medics, organiser's staff – and a different crop of guests, local media and promotional staff turn up at each event.

If you were parachuted into the paddock with no knowledge of MotoGP, you would notice that everybody's shirt carries the name of the company they work for and further observation would show that there is often some sort of colour coding. Some Japanese factory staff wear much plainer shirts than others, indicating that they're not attached to any particular ►

▶ team. A few Dorna people wear white shirts rather than the usual polo shirts – they're the head honchos.

At the track or on TV, you see the rider and perhaps the team owner and a mechanic or two, but behind the garage door every rider has engineers from tyre, suspension and brake companies looking after him. Within the team there will be physios, drivers, chefs, hospitality staff and press officers, plus promotional staff generating a bit of sales revenue in the public areas.

The hierarchy is complex. Dorna leases the rights to the championship from the FIM, the governing body of motorcycle sport worldwide, and then Dorna contracts IRTA, the International Racing Teams Association, to provide the show. IRTA, whose people wear blue shirts, organises the racing and polices the paddock. Representatives from the FIM, Dorna and IRTA make up Race Direction, the committee responsible for the big decisions on race weekends.

MotoGP also attracts the attention of the celebrity world. Brad Pitt has been seen at Laguna Seca, actors Ewan McGregor and Daniel Day Lewis are serious motorcycle racing fans. Several million pounds worth of footballer have been seen in the paddocks of Barcelona, Valencia and Rio. Mark Knopfler has been spotted lurking discretely at Donington Park. There was nearly a riot when American icon Michael Jordan turned up at Valencia for the first time.

It's good for MotoGP to have such world stars in the paddock, but the sport takes the precaution of bringing its own superstars to the races every time.

◀ Just like any weekend in the main street of your local town, only this is the main thoroughfare of the paddock.
ANDREW NORTHCOTT

▼ There's no getting away from the fact that motorcycle racing – and motorcycle racers – attract beautiful women. This lady, you wont be surprised to learn, is a famous Italian model.
MILAGRO

◀◀ MotoGP's ever-increasing profile has attracted interest from other sports. Michael Schumacher rode his Harley down to the 2006 Mugello race.
ANDREW NORTHCOTT

◀ American icon Michael 'Air' Jordan greets the new American Champion, Nicky Hayden. It's worth remembering while looking at this picture that Nicky is far from being the smallest guy on the grid.
ANDREW NORTHCOTT

▼ At flyaway races, bikes, equipment and other paraphernalia of paddock life have to travel in flight boxes and often have to move on to a race the following weekend. This is the Jacarepagua paddock just an hour or two after the end of the Rio GP, with most of the cases ready to go to the airport.

MILAGRO

► Even in a closed paddock it can be difficult for Valentino to get to work. When paddock passes are sold, as they are at Motegi and Laguna Seca, the security guys can have a hard day's work on their hands.

MILAGRO

YAMAHA
MOTUL
KERA
FASTI
IMAT
R.C., IN
CAMEL
DAINESE
46
YAMAHA
IL
AUREA
agv
Valentino

▼Some pictures are crying out for a caption. Mick Doohan observes Valentino Rossi's pre-race contortions and thinks 'Jeez mate, we didn't have to do all that stuff in my day.'

PAUL BARSHON

◄The Italian midsummer ritual of Water Day is an excuse for all sorts of reprehensible behaviour.

SHIGEO KIBIKI

► John Hopkins' parents were British so perhaps we shouldn't be surprised to find him scanning the *Daily Mirror* in an off-duty moment.

ANDREW NORTHCOTT

This sort of crash-zoom shot only works if there's a point of interest that's in sharp focus. This photo works perfectly because it's the rider who's in focus while the pit garage around him dissolves in a blur of activity.

GOLD AND GOOSE

▲A study in concentration and precision: a Team d'Antin mechanic works on the brake callipers of Shinya Nakano's Yamaha M1.

GOLD AND GOOSE

▲The first MotoGP race at Laguna Seca set a new record for celebrities in the paddock, with Brad Pitt being the most famous face to put in an appearance.

GIORGIO NEYROZ

► Sometimes the paddock can seem even more like a mobile village than usual: leathers hung out to air on the first floor of Rio's makeshift pit buildings look like washing waving in the wind.
GIORGIO NEYROZ

► The sponsor's promotions girl looks happy in her work – even if Valentino has decided to make her the first target of his celebratory cava.
MILAGRO

▼A racer just can't resist a challenge. When Ducati decided that the paddock really needed a mechanical rodeo bull, Nicky Hayden just had to play the cowboy.
ANDREW NORTHCOTT

▼Lots of celebrities great and small get to sample the delights of the two-seater MotoGP Ducati piloted by Randy Mamola. Football legend Gabriel Batistuta, Argentina's most prolific scorer, was suitably impressed.
GIORGIO NEYROZ

►MotoGP mechanics don't have nine-to-five jobs. The race finished hours ago but the Kawasaki team will be testing the next day so the work goes on.
GOLD AND GOOSE

18
Kawasaki
Ninja
G-SHOCK
AFAM
BRIDGESTONE

movistar
Telefónica
BLACK PRINCE
Castrol
Arai
polini
74
SPIDI

◀ Jerez 2005 and Valentino Rossi has just shoved Sete Gibernau out of the way at the final corner. Now he proffers the hand of friendship but the Spaniard takes his time about accepting it. You know very well from the body language in this photo who won and who lost.

ANDREW NORTHCOTT

WINNING & LOSING

Most racers find it difficult to treat those two imposters just the same

A surprisingly small number of riders won a MotoGP race under the 990cc regulations. Valentino Rossi, of course, won both on a Honda and a Yamaha, as did Max Biaggi. They're the only two riders to have won on the M1. On the other hand, Honda's V5 RC211V also carried Tohru Ukawa, Alex Barros, Sete Gibernau, Makoto Tamada, Nicky Hayden, Marco Melandri, Dani Pedrosa and Toni Elias to victory. The works 990cc Ducati Desmosedici was only ever ridden by four riders and two of them – Loris Capirossi and Troy Bayliss – won on it.

So just a dozen men have stood on top of a MotoGP rostrum and three of them have done it just once, two of them twice.

Which makes Valentino Rossi's tally of 45 wins from ▶

▶ the 82 races of the 990 years all the more remarkable. No-one else has managed to get near double figures.

Sete Gibernau is second in the rankings with eight wins. He's one of very few riders to have beaten Rossi when there were no weather or machinery factors to distort the picture. His 2003 victories in South Africa and Germany were especially praiseworthy. Max Biaggi never put a sustained championship campaign together, but with hindsight his two wins in the first year of MotoGP look better and better. The Yamaha didn't win again until Rossi got on it.

The only non-Japanese factory to win was Ducati wtih seven victories, all but one of them thanks to Loris Capirossi. The comparatively tiny Italian factory was competitive from its first race – Capirossi and Troy Bayliss were first and fifth at Suzuka 2003. The Aussie neatly topped and tailed the 990 Ducati project by winning the very last race under the formula.

Every racer thinks he's the fastest man out there – he wouldn't be there if he didn't – which makes dealing with defeat doubly difficult. Some cope with it better than others. They all know the rules: first you must beat your team-mate, then you must beat your fellow countrymen, and only after that can you start thinking about winning the race. All of them know very well that second place means you are the first loser.

◀ Toni Elias and his race engineer Fabrizio Cecchini celebrate victory in the 2006 Portuguese GP, one of the most dramatic races of the 990 era. Cecchini was previously race engineer for Daijiro Kato.
MARTIN HEATH

▲ Makoto Tamada flies the Japanese flag, and the Motegi marshals fly any flag they can lay their hands on to celebrate victory in the 2004 Japanese GP. It was the second of Tamada's two wins.
GOLD AND GOOSE

▼At the end of the 2002 season Alex Barros got a Honda V5 for four races, won two of them and got on the rostrum in the other two. Team boss Sito Pons embraces his rider after his brilliant win at Valencia, where Alex swapped the lead twice with Rossi on the final lap.

ANDREW NORTHCOTT

►In 2003 Alex Barros joined the factory Yamaha team and looked set to be a championship contender. He was very fast in testing but sustained a nasty injury in the very first practice session of the year and only managed one rostrum finish all year. That is the look of despair.

ANDREW NORTHCOTT

▼Max Biaggi celebrates his win at the 2004 Sachsenring German GP, which would turn out to be the last of his five MotoGP victories. He won two races on the Yamaha M1 and three on the Honda RC211V.

GOLD AND GOOSE

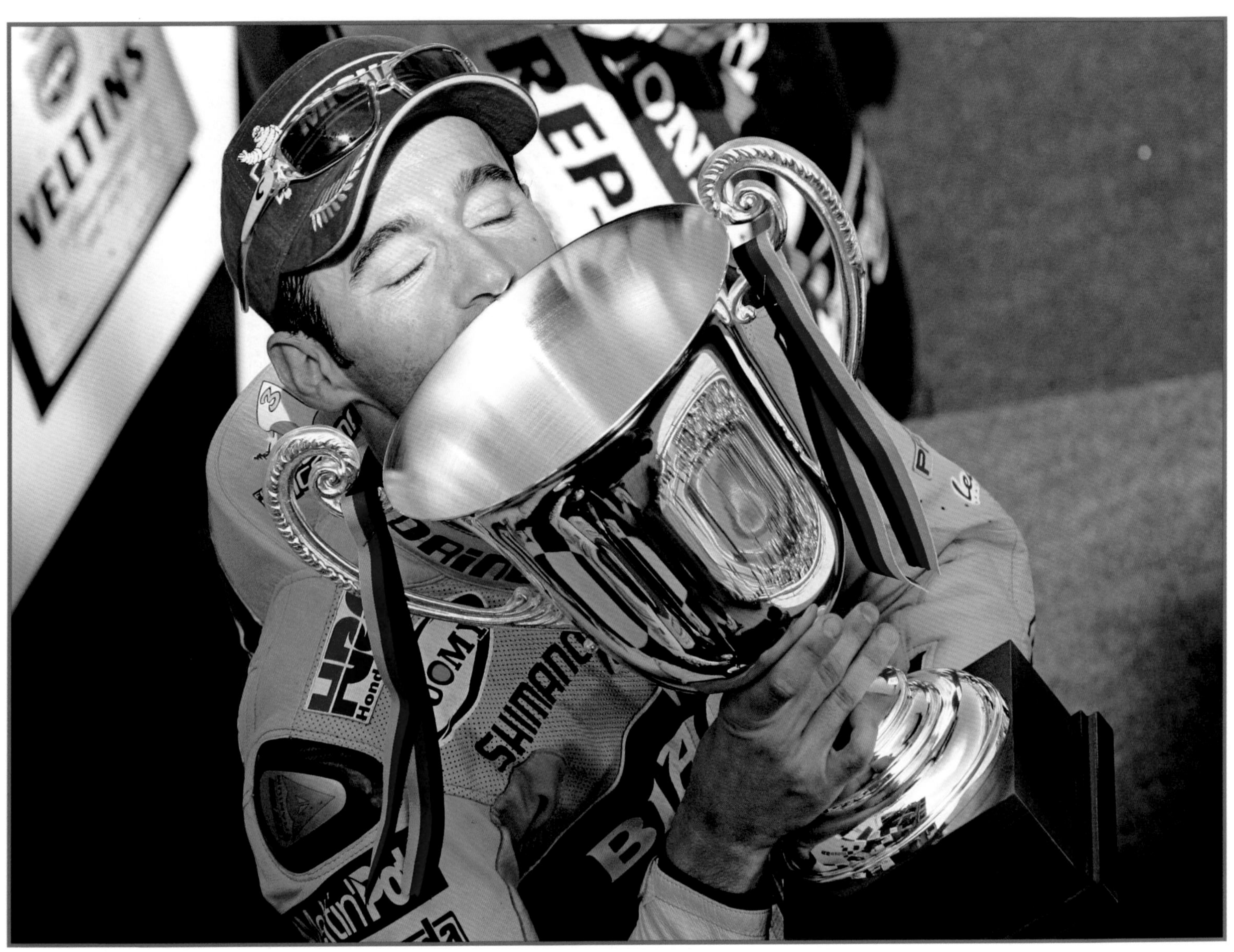

▼ Biaggi has to look on as Rossi holds the trophy for the 2004 South African GP. Most people remember that this was Valentino's first race on the Yamaha, and tend to forget he only won it after an epic battle with Max.
GOLD AND GOOSE

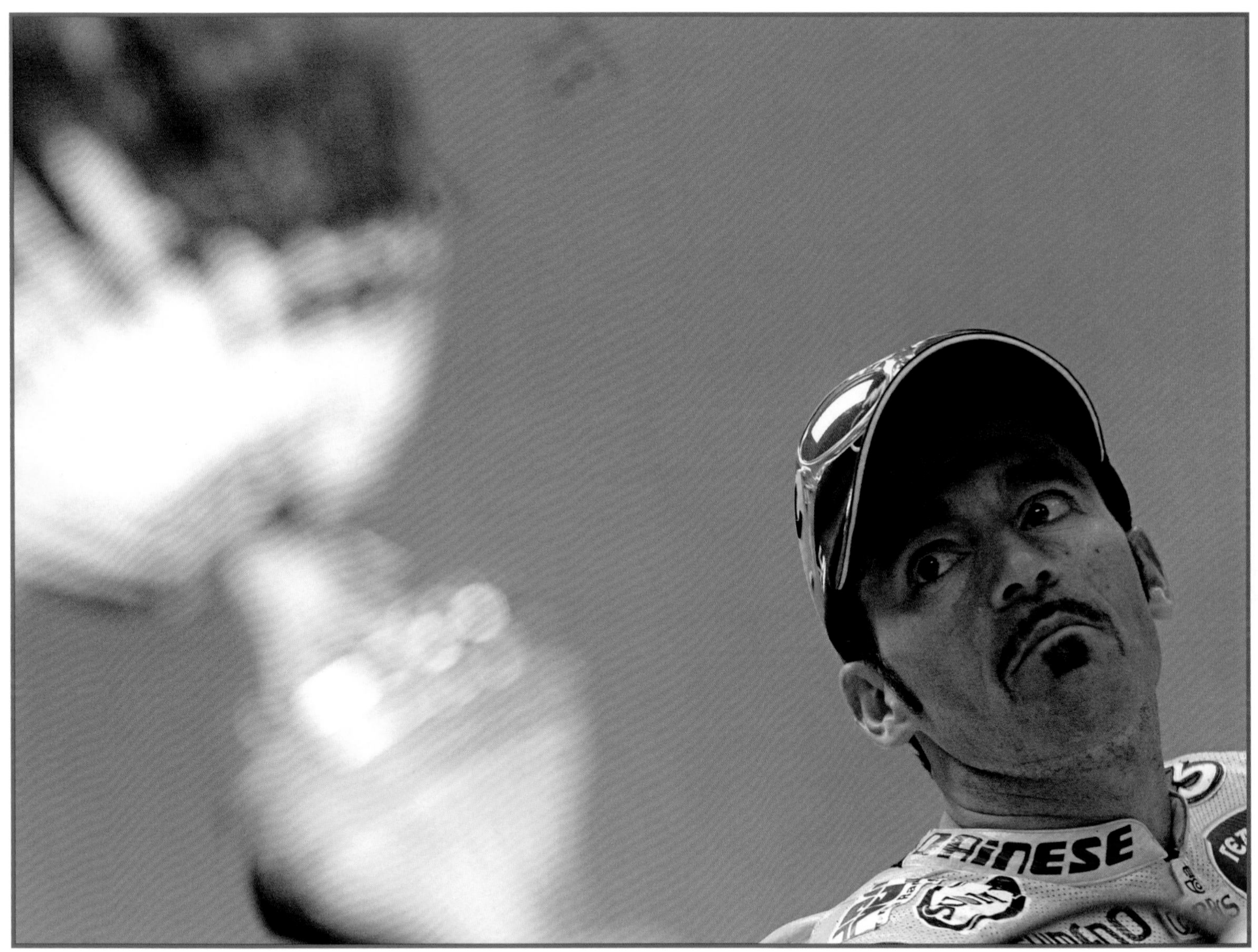

▼ Sete Gibernau was the second most successful rider of the 990 era with eight wins, all of them for the Gresini Honda team. This celebration is from Le Mans, the only track where he won twice.

ANDREW NORTHCOTT

▶ When a rider loses, his team loses too. With Rossi and his posse celebrating behind them, Gibernau's mechanics look like they'd rather be anywhere else in the world than parc fermé.

MARTIN HEATH

▲ Sete Gibernau gives vent to his frustration in a Jerez gravel trap after crashing while second in the 2003 Spanish GP. It was only the third race of the year and Sete knew he'd just gifted Rossi a crucial points advantage.
PAUL BARSHON

Í VARUJE:
OVINU.
MINISTERSTVO ZDRAVOTNICTVÍ
KOUŘENÍ ZPŮSOBUJE RAKO
GAUL
ĚRSTVO ZDRAVOTN
NÍ ZPŮSOBUJE
MINISTERS
KOUŘENÍ
MINIS
KOUŘ
BRIDGESTONE
Alice
ADVANCE
DUCATI CORSE
SUOMY
OAKLEY
motogp
DUCATI
BRNO CIRCUIT
CZECH REPUBLIC

◄ Finally free from the injuries caused by the Barcelona crash, Loris Capirossi has won the 2006 Czech GP and knows that he can still do what matters most to him – win. Six victories make him the third most successful man of the 990 years.
GARETH HARFORD

▲ Marco Melandri seems a little surprised by the size of his trophy for winning the 2006 Turkish GP. He won both races at the Istanbul Park circuit and a total of five on 990s.
GOLD AND GOOSE

▼What better way to celebrate another win than to send a Michelin slick to smoky oblivion?
MIRCO LAZZARI

▼2006 Rookie of the Year Dani Pedrosa won two races in 2006. He came to MotoGP with better career statistics than Rossi in the 125 and 250 classes, and his first MotoGP win – in China – made him the youngest ever to win in all three classes of GP motorcycle racing.
ANDREW NORTHCOTT

▶Valentino Rossi celebrates what many consider his greatest win, the Australian GP of 2003 when he overcame a ten-second penalty. He thought it may have been the only time he went at 100% for a whole race. His banner was in tribute to Barry Sheene.
ANDREW NORTHCOTT

SKYY VODKA
SKYY VODKA
7
REPSOL
GAS
GASJEANS.COM
HONDA
GREAT WHITE
Dainese
REPSOL
SKYY VODKA
SKYY VODKA
Phill

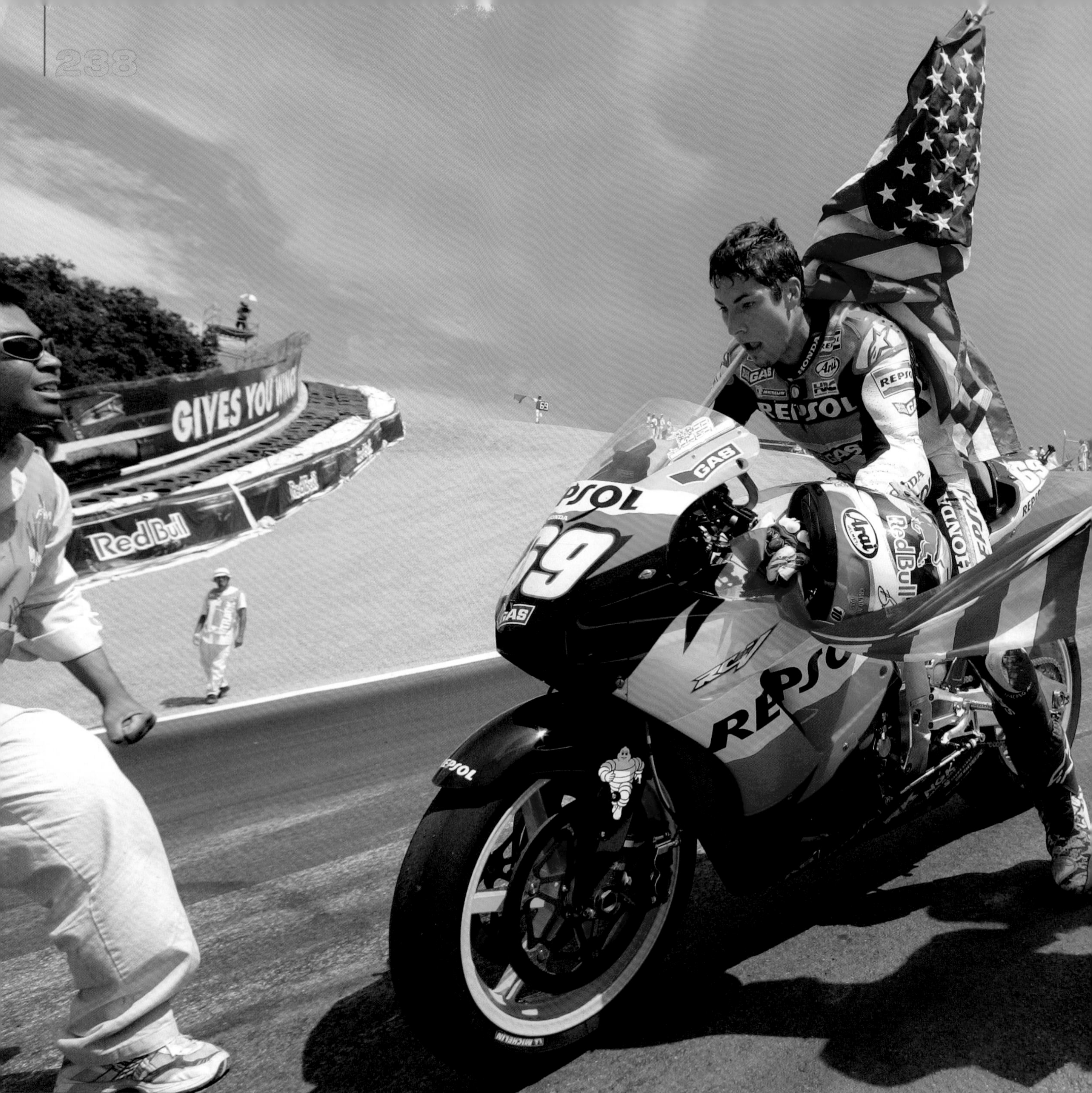

▲ Back in the USA: MotoGP returned to Laguna Seca in 2005 and local hero Nicky Hayden won. He won again in 2006, and this striking photo was taken on the slow-down lap. Nicky went on to become World Champion, the only racer other than Rossi to wear the MotoGP crown between 2002 and 2006.
GOLD AND GOOSE

► The very last race under 990cc rules was won by Troy Bayliss, who then announced that it had been his final MotoGP appearance. It was Troy's only victory and also the only win by a wild-card or replacement rider (he was standing in for the injured Sete Gibernau). He was also the oldest rider to win a 990 race.
ANDREW NORTHCOTT

▲ Tohru Ukawa was Rossi's team-mate in the Repsol Honda team in the first year of MotoGP. He won the South African GP – his only MotoGP win – after a last-lap showdown with the Italian.

GOLD AND GOOSE

RESULTS 2002-2006

2002

	Rider	Nation	Motorcycle	Japan	South Africa	Spain	France	Italy	Catalunya	The Netherlands	Great Britain	Germany	Czech Republic	Portugal	Rio	Pacific	Malaysia	Australia	Valencia	Points
1	**Rossi**	ITA	**Honda**	25	20	25	25	25	25	25	25	25	–	25	25	20	20	25	20	**355**
2	**Biaggi**	ITA	**Yamaha**	–	7	–	16	20	13	13	20	20	25	10	20	–	25	10	16	**215**
3	**Ukawa**	JPN	**Honda**	–	25	16	20	16	20	11	–	16	16	16	–	13	13	16	11	**209**
4	**Barros**	BRA	**Honda**	10	–	11	8	11	11	20	16	–	7	11	13	25	16	20	25	**204**
5	**Checa**	SPA	**Yamaha**	16	11	–	–	13	16	16	–	13	11	20	–	11	9	5	–	**141**
6	**Abe**	JPN	**Yamaha**	11	9	10	13	9	–	7	13	10	8	9	10	8	6	–	6	**129**
7	**Kato**	JPN	**Honda**	6	13	20	–	–	8	4	9	–	20	–	–	–	11	13	13	**117**
8	**Capirossi**	ITA	**Honda**	7	16	13	9	10	10	–	–	–	10	–	11	16	7	–	–	**109**
9	**Roberts**	USA	**Suzuki**	–	–	8	11	–	9	10	2	–	5	13	16	10	8	7	–	**99**
10	**Jacque**	FRA	**Yamaha**	–	10	5	–	7	7	2	11	–	6	–	9	9	–	8	7	**81**
11	**Nakano**	JPN	**Yamaha**	–	8	–	3	5	–	8	6	11	–	4	–	–	10	3	10	**68**
12	**Aoki**	JPN	**Proton KR**	9	–	9	10	–	–	–	7	8	–	–	4	7	–	9	–	**63**
13	**vd Goorbergh**	NED	**Honda**	–	5	4	1	2	–	6	1	4	4	–	7	3	3	11	9	**60**
14	**McWilliams**	GBR	**Proton KR**	–	–	–	6	–	4	–	–	9	9	7	–	6	4	6	8	**59**
15	**Hopkins**	USA	**Yamaha**	4	2	3	5	4	6	9	8	–	–	8	2	2	–	–	5	**58**
16	**Gibernau**	SPA	**Suzuki**	–	–	7	4	–	–	–	10	–	13	–	8	–	2	4	3	**51**
17	**Harada**	JPN	**Honda**	5	4	6	–	6	3	3	5	–	1	6	3	1	–	2	2	**47**
18	**Ryo**	JPN	**Suzuki**	20	–	–	–	–	5	1	3	5	2	–	–	–	5	–	–	**41**
19	**Laconi**	FRA	**Aprilia**	8	1	2	7	8	2	–	–	–	–	–	–	5	–	–	–	**33**
20	**McCoy**	AUS	**Yamaha**	–	6	1	–	–	–	–	4	7	3	5	6	–	1	–	–	**33**
21	**Itoh**	JPN	**Honda**	13	–	–	–	–	–	–	–	–	–	–	–	–	–	–	–	**13**
22	**Hofmann**	GER	**Yamaha**	–	–	–	–	–	–	5	–	6	–	–	–	–	–	–	–	**11**
23	**Cardoso**	SPA	**Yamaha**	–	–	–	–	–	–	–	–	3	–	–	5	–	–	1	–	**9**
24	**Bayle**	FRA	**Yamaha**	–	–	–	2	3	–	–	–	–	–	–	–	–	–	–	–	**5**
25	**Yoshikawa**	JPN	**Yamaha**	–	–	–	–	–	–	–	–	–	–	–	–	4	–	–	–	**4**
26	**Pitt**	AUS	**Kawasaki**	–	–	–	–	–	–	–	–	–	–	–	–	–	–	–	4	**4**
27	**Riba**	SPA	**Yamaha**	–	3	–	–	–	1	–	–	–	–	–	–	–	–	–	–	**4**

2003

	Rider	Nation	Motorcycle	Japan	South Africa	Spain	France	Italy	Catalunya	The Netherlands	Great Britain	Germany	Czech Republic	Portugal	Rio	Pacific	Malaysia	Australia	Valencia	Points
1	**Rossi**	ITA	**Honda**	25	20	25	20	25	20	16	16	20	25	25	25	20	25	25	25	**357**
2	**Gibernau**	SPA	**Honda**	13	25	–	25	9	16	25	20	25	20	13	20	13	20	13	20	**277**
3	**Biaggi**	ITA	**Honda**	20	16	20	11	16	2	20	25	–	11	20	13	25	16	–	13	**228**
4	**Capirossi**	ITA	**Ducati**	16	–	–	–	20	25	10	13	13	–	16	10	8	10	20	16	**177**
5	**Hayden**	USA	**Honda**	9	9	–	4	4	7	5	8	11	10	7	11	16	13	16	–	**130**
6	**Bayliss**	AUS	**Ducati**	11	13	16	–	–	6	7	11	16	16	10	6	–	7	–	9	**128**
7	**Checa**	SPA	**Yamaha**	6	7	–	–	8	13	13	10	8	13	8	7	–	11	8	11	**123**
8	**Ukawa**	JPN	**Honda**	–	10	13	9	10	10	4	–	10	8	11	9	9	9	11	–	**123**
9	**Barros**	BRA	**Yamaha**	8	11	11	16	–	8	8	–	–	9	5	4	10	1	–	10	**101**
10	**Nakano**	JPN	**Yamaha**	7	5	8	2	11	11	3	7	9	2	4	8	7	8	9	–	**101**
11	**Tamada**	JPN	**Honda**	–	2	10	–	13	9	–	3	3	7	6	16	–	6	6	6	**87**
12	**Jacque**	FRA	**Yamaha**	1	6	6	13	6	–	11	–	7	5	3	–	3	–	10	–	**71**
13	**Edwards**	USA	**Aprilia**	10	–	2	6	7	–	9	6	2	4	2	3	–	3	–	8	**62**
14	**Haga**	JPN	**Aprilia**	4	–	5	8	–	4	–	9	–	3	1	2	4	4	2	1	**47**
15	**Melandri**	ITA	**Yamaha**	–	–	–	1	5	3	–	–	–	6	9	5	11	5	–	–	**45**
16	**Abe**	JPN	**Yamaha**	5	8	–	5	–	–	–	–	6	–	–	–	–	–	–	7	**31**
17	**Hopkins**	USA	**Suzuki**	3	3	9	–	–	1	1	5	–	–	–	–	–	–	4	3	**29**
18	**McWilliams**	GBR	**Proton KR**	–	–	4	10	–	–	–	–	4	–	–	–	–	–	5	4	**27**
19	**Roberts**	USA	**Suzuki**	2	1	3	–	–	–	–	–	1	–	–	–	1	2	7	5	**22**
20	**Kiyonari**	JPN	**Honda**	–	–	–	3	3	5	–	2	–	1	–	–	1	5	–	2	**22**
21	**Aoki**	JPN	**Proton KR**	–	4	7	–	–	–	–	1	5	–	–	–	2	–	–	–	**19**
22	**McCoy**	AUS	**Kawasaki**	–	–	–	7	1	–	–	–	–	–	–	–	–	–	3	–	**11**
23	**Hofmann**	GER	**Kawasaki**	–	–	–	–	2	–	6	–	–	–	–	–	–	–	–	–	**8**
24	**Ryo**	JPN	**Suzuki**	–	–	–	–	–	–	–	–	–	–	–	–	6	–	–	–	**6**
25	**Kagayama**	JPN	**Suzuki**	–	–	–	–	–	–	–	4	–	–	–	–	–	–	–	–	**4**
26	**Pitt**	AUS	**Kawasaki**	–	–	1	–	–	–	2	–	–	–	–	–	–	–	1	–	**4**

2004

	Rider	Nation	Motorcycle	South Africa	Spain	France	Italy	Catalunya	The Netherlands	Rio	Germany	Great Britain	Czech Republic	Portugal	Japan	Qatar	Malaysia	Australia	Valencia	Points
1	**Rossi**	ITA	**Yamaha**	25	13	13	25	25	25	–	13	25	20	25	20	–	25	25	25	**304**
2	**Gibernau**	SPA	**Honda**	16	25	25	20	20	20	–	–	16	25	13	10	25	9	20	13	**257**
3	**Biaggi**	ITA	**Honda**	20	20	16	16	8	13	20	25	4	16	–	–	10	20	9	20	**217**
4	**Barros**	BRA	**Honda**	13	16	9	10	–	–	11	20	7	–	16	13	13	16	11	10	**165**
5	**Edwards**	USA	**Honda**	9	9	11	4	11	10	10	11	20	9	7	–	20	5	13	8	**157**
6	**Tamada**	JPN	**Honda**	8	–	7	–	–	4	25	10	2	13	20	25	6	11	8	11	**150**
7	**Checa**	SPA	**Yamaha**	6	10	20	–	13	7	6	–	10	10	11	9	–	7	6	2	**117**
8	**Hayden**	USA	**Honda**	11	11	5	–	–	11	16	16	13	–	–	–	11	13	10	–	**117**
9	**Capirossi**	ITA	**Ducati**	10	4	6	8	6	8	13	–	9	11	9	–	–	10	16	7	**117**
10	**Nakano**	JPN	**Kawasaki**	4	7	–	–	9	–	7	9	1	4	5	16	–	8	4	9	**83**
11	**Xaus**	SPA	**Ducati**	–	–	2	11	10	9	4	5	5	–	–	7	16	3	5	–	**77**
12	**Melandri**	ITA	**Yamaha**	5	–	10	7	16	16	3	–	–	7	–	11	–	–	–	–	**75**
13	**Abe**	JPN	**Yamaha**	7	5	–	9	7	5	8	–	–	8	6	–	9	4	–	6	**74**
14	**Bayliss**	AUS	**Ducati**	2	–	8	13	–	–	–	–	11	–	8	–	–	6	7	16	**71**
15	**Hofmann**	GER	**Kawasaki**	–	3	–	2	5	3	5	6	–	3	3	6	7	–	3	5	**51**
16	**Hopkins**	USA	**Suzuki**	3	1	–	–	–	2	1	7	8	–	10	–	8	–	1	4	**45**
17	**Hodgson**	GBR	**Ducati**	–	–	–	5	4	6	–	3	6	5	–	8	–	–	–	1	**38**
18	**Ke. Roberts**	USA	**Suzuki**	–	8	4	–	–	–	9	8	–	6	2	–	–	–	–	–	**37**
19	**McWilliams**	GBR	**Aprilia**	–	–	3	–	–	1	2	4	–	2	4	4	–	1	2	3	**26**
20	**Byrne**	GBR	**Aprilia**	1	–	–	6	3	–	–	2	3	–	–	3	–	–	–	–	**18**
21	**Aoki**	JPN	**Proton KR**	–	2	–	3	1	–	–	–	–	1	1	2	–	–	–	–	**10**
22	**Fabrizio**	ITA	**WCM**	–	6	–	1	–	–	–	1	–	–	–	–	–	–	–	–	**8**
23	**Kagayama**	JPN	**Suzuki**	–	–	–	–	–	–	–	–	–	–	–	–	5	2	–	–	**7**
24	**Jacque**	FRA	**Moriwaki**	–	–	–	–	–	–	–	–	–	–	–	5	–	–	–	–	**5**
25	**Haydon**	GBR	**Proton KR**	–	–	–	–	–	–	–	–	–	–	–	–	4	–	–	–	**4**
26	**Ellison**	GBR	**WCM**	–	–	–	–	–	–	–	–	–	–	–	–	3	–	–	–	**3**
27	**Pitt**	AUS	**Moriwaki**	–	–	–	–	2	–	–	–	–	–	–	–	–	–	–	–	**2**
0	**Ui**	JPN	**WCM**	–	–	–	–	–	–	–	–	–	–	–	1	–	–	–	–	**1**
0	**Ku. Roberts**	USA	**Proton KR**	–	–	1	–	–	–	–	–	–	–	–	–	–	–	–	–	**1**

2005

	Rider	Nation	Motorcycle	Spain	Portugal	China	France	Italy	Catalunya	The Netherlands	United States	Great Britain	Germany	Czech Republic	Japan	Malaysia	Qatar	Australia	Turkey	Valencia	Points
1	**Rossi**	ITA	**Yamaha**	25	20	25	25	25	25	25	16	25	25	25	–	20	25	25	20	16	**367**
2	**Melandri**	ITA	**Honda**	16	13	16	13	13	16	20	–	–	9	10	–	11	20	13	25	25	**220**
3	**Hayden**	USA	**Honda**	–	9	7	10	10	11	13	25	–	16	11	9	13	16	20	16	20	**206**
4	**Edwards**	USA	**Yamaha**	7	10	8	16	7	9	16	20	13	8	9	10	6	13	10	9	8	**179**
5	**Biaggi**	ITA	**Honda**	9	16	11	11	20	10	10	13	–	13	16	20	10	–	–	4	10	**173**
6	**Capirossi**	ITA	**Ducati**	3	7	4	9	16	4	6	6	10	7	20	25	25	6	–	–	9	**157**
7	**Gibernau**	SPA	**Honda**	20	–	13	20	–	20	11	11	–	20	–	–	–	11	11	13	–	**150**
8	**Barros**	BRA	**Honda**	13	25	5	–	9	13	9	–	16	11	13	–	8	7	–	7	11	**147**
9	**C. Checa**	SPA	**Ducati**	6	11	–	–	11	5	7	–	11	–	8	13	16	10	16	11	13	**138**
10	**Nakano**	JPN	**Kawasaki**	11	8	–	8	6	7	8	7	–	10	4	–	–	9	9	6	5	**98**
11	**Tamada**	JPN	**Honda**	8	–	–	–	8	–	2	9	9	6	6	16	4	–	8	8	7	**91**
12	**Elias**	SPA	**Yamaha**	4	2	2	7	–	–	–	3	7	4	2	7	5	8	7	10	6	**74**
13	**Roberts**	USA	**Suzuki**	–	4	–	3	1	1	–	2	20	5	5	8	9	5	–	–	–	**63**
14	**Hopkins**	USA	**Suzuki**	2	–	9	–	5	–	3	8	5	–	3	11	7	–	6	1	3	**63**
15	**Bayliss**	AUS	**Honda**	10	5	–	6	3	8	5	10	–	–	7	–	–	–	–	–	–	**54**
16	**Xaus**	SPA	**Yamaha**	–	6	6	4	2	6	4	5	–	3	–	6	1	2	4	2	1	**52**
17	**Jacque**	FRA	**Kawasaki**	–	–	20	5	–	–	–	–	–	–	–	–	–	–	–	3	–	**28**
18	**Rolfo**	ITA	**Ducati**	1	3	–	1	–	2	–	–	6	2	–	–	3	4	3	–	–	**25**
19	**Hofmann**	GER	**Kawasaki**	5	–	–	–	4	–	–	4	8	–	1	–	–	–	–	–	2	**24**
20	**vd Goorbergh**	NED	**Honda**	–	–	10	2	–	–	–	–	–	–	–	–	–	–	–	–	–	**12**
21	**Vermeulen**	AUS	**Honda**	–	–	–	–	–	–	–	–	–	–	–	–	–	–	5	5	–	**10**
22	**Battaini**	ITA	**WCM**	–	–	–	–	–	–	–	–	–	1	–	5	–	–	1	–	–	**7**
23	**Ellison**	GBR	**WCM**	–	1	3	–	–	–	–	–	–	–	–	–	–	1	2	–	–	**7**
24	**Byrne**	GBR	**Proton KR**	–	–	–	–	–	–	–	1	–	–	–	–	2	3	–	–	–	**6**
25	**Kiyonari**	JPN	**Honda**	–	–	–	–	–	–	–	–	–	–	–	–	–	–	–	–	4	**4**
26	**D. Checa**	SPA	**Yamaha**	–	–	–	–	–	3	1	–	–	–	–	–	–	–	–	–	–	**4**
27	**Ukawa**	JPN	**Moriwaki**	–	–	1	–	–	–	–	–	–	–	–	–	–	–	–	–	–	**1**

2006

	Rider	Nation	Motorcycle	Spain	Qatar	Turkey	China	France	Italy	Catalunya	The Netherlands	Great Britain	Germany	United States	Czech Republic	Malaysia	Australia	Japan	Portugal	Valencia	Points
1	**Hayden**	USA	**Honda**	16	20	16	20	11	16	20	25	9	16	25	7	13	11	11	–	16	**252**
2	**Rossi**	ITA	**Yamaha**	2	25	13	–	–	25	25	8	20	25	–	20	25	16	20	20	3	**247**
3	**Capirossi**	ITA	**Ducati**	25	16	10	8	20	20	–	1	7	11	8	25	20	9	25	4	20	**229**
4	**Melandri**	ITA	**Honda**	11	9	25	9	25	10	–	9	16	20	16	11	7	25	16	8	11	**228**
5	**Pedrosa**	SPA	**Honda**	20	10	2	25	16	13	–	16	25	13	20	16	16	1	9	–	13	**215**
6	**Roberts**	USA	**KR211V**	8	6	3	3	–	8	16	11	11	–	13	13	9	2	7	16	8	**134**
7	**Edwards**	USA	**Yamaha**	5	7	7	16	10	4	11	3	10	4	7	6	6	–	8	13	7	**124**
8	**Stoner**	AUS	**Honda**	10	11	20	11	13	–	–	13	13	–	–	10	8	10	–	–	–	**119**
9	**Elias**	SPA	**Honda**	13	8	11	5	7	9	–	–	–	5	1	5	–	7	10	25	10	**116**
10	**Hopkins**	USA	**Suzuki**	7	–	–	13	1	6	13	10	8	6	10	9	10	4	4	10	5	**116**
11	**Vermeulen**	AUS	**Suzuki**	4	–	9	–	6	2	10	6	–	9	11	4	5	20	5	7	–	**98**
12	**Tamada**	JPN	**Honda**	6	2	6	10	9	7	9	5	5	–	5	3	2	6	6	11	4	**96**
13	**Gibernau**	SPA	**Honda**	–	13	5	7	8	11	–	–	–	8	6	–	11	13	13	–	–	**95**
14	**Nakano**	JPN	**Kawasaki**	9	5	8	6	4	5	–	20	–	10	–	8	–	8	–	–	9	**92**
15	**Checa**	SPA	**Yamaha**	3	4	1	2	5	1	8	7	6	7	9	1	4	–	2	9	6	**75**
16	**De Puniet**	FRA	**Kawasaki**	–	–	4	4	–	3	–	2	4	–	4	2	3	5	–	6	–	**37**
17	**Hofmann**	GER	**Ducati**	1	1	–	1	3	–	6	4	3	–	2	–	1	3	–	5	–	**30**
18	**Ellison**	GBR	**Yamaha**	–	3	–	–	2	–	7	–	2	3	3	–	–	–	1	3	2	**26**
19	**Bayliss**	AUS	**Ducati**	–	–	–	–	–	–	–	–	–	–	–	–	–	–	–	–	25	**25**
20	**Cardoso**	SPA	**Ducati**	–	–	–	–	–	–	5	–	1	2	–	–	–	–	–	2	–	**10**
21	**Akiyoshi**	JPN	**Suzuki**	–	–	–	–	–	–	–	–	–	–	–	–	–	–	3	–	–	**3**
22	**McCoy**	AUS	**Ilmor SRT**	–	–	–	–	–	–	–	–	–	–	–	–	–	–	–	1	1	**2**